A LEGACY
OF PROMISES
for a Godly Man

SELECTED WRITINGS FROM

Max Lucado

Jack Hayford

Charles Swindoll

Tony Evans

and others

Copyright © 1998 by Promise Keepers

Published by J. Countryman ® a Division of Thomas
Nelson, Inc., Nashville, Tennessee 37214.

Managing editor—Terri Gibbs
Project editors—Deborah Mendenhall, Mary Guenther

A J. Countryman ® Book

Designed by Koechel Peterson, and Associates, Inc.
Minneapolis, Minnesota

ISBN: 08499-5438-X

Printed in Belgium

CONTENTS

A Man and His God. 7

Worshiping God
Prayer
Obeying to God's Word
Disciplined Spirituality

A Man and His Friends. 43

Friendship with Christian Brothers
Accountability to Christian Brothers

A Man and His Integrity. 63

Sexual Purity
Moral Conduct
Ethical Principles

A Man and His Family. 87

Committed to Your Wife
Faithful to Your Wife
Honoring Your Wife
Providing Spiritual Guidance for Your Family
Providing Protection for Your Family
Disciplining Your Children

A Man and His Church. 133

Honoring and Supporting Your Pastor
Giving of Time and Resources

A Man and His Brothers. 145

Reconciled to Christ
Reconciled with Your Brothers
Unity in the Body

A Man and His World. 165

Sharing the Good News with Others
Reaching Out to the World

A MAN AND HIS GOD

WORSHIPING GOD

We are ambassadors for Christ, as though God were pleading through us: we implore you on Christ's behalf, be reconciled to God. For He made Him who knew no sin to be sin for us, that we might become the righteousness of God in Him.

2 CORINTHIANS 5:20–21

Who is a God like You,
Pardoning iniquity
And passing over the transgression
*   of the remnant of His heritage?*
You will cast all our sins
Into the depths of the sea.

MICAH 7:18, 19

He who did not spare His own Son, but delivered Him up for us all, how shall He not with Him also freely give us all things?

ROMANS 8:32

YOU HAVE EVERYTHING IN JESUS

Once there was a wealthy man whose son preceded him in death. The rich man had a photo of his son whom he loved very much. When the man died, his belongings were gathered to be sold at an auction. The auctioneer said that the first thing they would auction was that picture. But no one bid on it. They were waiting for everything else. . . .

When no one would bid on the photo, the auctioneer explained that the man's will stated that the picture of his son had to go before anything else could be auctioned. Finally, one man said, "I bid a dollar."

The auctioneer said, "A dollar . . . going once, going twice . . . sold for a dollar!" Then he said, "Now this auction is closed."

Everybody got upset, but the auctioneer explained. In his will the wealthy man had determined that whoever bid on the photo of his son would also receive his entire estate.

This is what I want to tell you. Maybe you've been going after this . . . after that. But . . . seek first the kingdom of God and all His righteousness and everything you need will be added unto you. You see, whoever gets the Son of God—Jesus Christ—gets everything else.

Jeffrey Johnson
(speech, Buffalo, New York, 1997)

WORSHIPING GOD

The world is passing away, and the lust of it; but he who does the will of God abides forever.

1 JOHN 2:17

Therefore humble yourselves under the mighty hand of God, that He may exalt you in due time.

1 PETER 5:6

As the Father loved Me, I also have loved you; abide in My love. If you keep My commandments, you will abide in My love, just as I have kept My Father's commandments and abide in His love.

JOHN 15:9-10

SUBMITTING TO THE WILL OF GOD

Many people don't understand this idea of gentleness or meekness. It has nothing to do with going around with your head down and your feet dragging. Meekness has to do with your . . . willingness to submit your will to the will of God.

The best example of meekness in action is the process of taming a wild stallion. The cowboy puts a saddle on this wild horse and gets on his back. The stallion bucks because he doesn't want to be ridden. The cowboy is determined to ride the stallion until he breaks him.

Is the cowboy trying to break the horse of its strength? No, he needs the horse's strength. Instead, he is trying to break the horse of its stubborn self-will. . . .

This is what God wants to do with you and me. He wants to bring our wills under His authority.

Tony Evans
What a Way to Live!

WORSHIPING GOD

And we know that all things work together for good to those who love God, to those who are the called according to His purpose.

ROMANS 8:28

Beloved, now we are children of God; and it has not yet been revealed what we shall be, but we know that when He is revealed, we shall be like Him, for we shall see Him as He is.

1 JOHN 3:2

By this we know love, because He laid down His life for us. And we also ought to lay down our lives for the brethren.

1 JOHN 3:16

AN ARK OF SAFETY

When the apostle Paul was a prisoner, he was en route by ship to Rome to appear before Caesar. The ship was caught in a storm and destroyed. We have an insight into a faithful God through reading the story. Obviously, many of the passengers could swim, but for those without life preservers, the Word notes, "some on boards, and some on broken pieces of the ship . . . they escaped all safe to land" (Acts 27:44).

When the ship broke up and the waves washed over the heads of those in the water, there were pieces of the ship, boards, and hatch covers to which they could cling, keeping them buoyant until they reached shore. Even in the most turbulent times God will always provide something for us to hold on to. He is like that. He promises pieces of safety in our storms, literally an ark of safety through His Son.

Wellington Boone
Breaking Through

WORSHIPING GOD

The kingdom of God is not eating and drinking, but righteousness and peace and joy in the Holy Spirit.

ROMANS 14:17

Behold what manner of love the Father has bestowed on us, that we should be called children of God! Therefore the world does not know us, because it did not know Him.

1 JOHN 3:1

Looking unto Jesus, the author and finisher of our faith, who for the joy that was set before Him endured the cross, despising the shame, and has sat down at the right hand of the throne of God. For consider Him who endured such hostility from sinners against Himself, lest you become weary and discouraged in your souls.

HEBREWS 12:2–3

GIVE GOD YOUR BEST

God paid a high price for you and me. We cost Him the life of His Son. Not only that, but He has entrusted us with the stewardship of His kingdom. He has given us the privilege of ruling with Him in His kingdom.

Are we going to turn around and give God sloppy work, our leftover time, talents, and treasure? Are we going to give the school district our best teaching efforts then throw something together on Saturday night to teach the kids at Sunday school?

Are we going to spend thousands of dollars on our houses and cars and clothes and then toss a little tip toward God? . . .

The Bible says whatever you get in time, talents, and treasure, make sure you give God His portion first. Because if you don't, you won't have any left over later.

Tony Evans
What a Way to Live!

PRAYER

Ask, and it will be given to you; seek, and you will find; knock, and it will be opened to you. For everyone who asks receives, and he who seeks finds, and to him who knocks it will be opened.

MATTHEW 7:7–8

Continue earnestly in prayer, being vigilant in it "with thanksgiving."

COLOSSIANS 4:2

Rejoicing in hope, patient in tribulation, continuing steadfastly in prayer.

ROMANS 12:12

And whatever things you ask in prayer, believing, you will receive.

MATTHEW 21:22

TAKING ON GOD'S HEART

In a happy home the husband doesn't talk to the wife only when he wants something from her. He doesn't pop in only when he wants a good meal or a clean shirt or a little romance. If he does, the home is not a home—it's a brothel that serves food and cleans clothes.

Healthy marriages have a sense of "remaining." The husband remains in the wife, and she remains in him. There is a tenderness, an honesty, an ongoing communication. The same is true in our relationship with God. Sometimes we go to God with our joys, and sometimes we go with our hurts, but we always go. And as we go, the more we go, the more we become like Him. . . .

As we walk with God, we take on His thoughts, His principles, His attitudes. We take on His heart.

Max Lucado
Just Like Jesus

PRAYER

Rejoice always, pray without ceasing, in everything give thanks for this is the will of God in Christ Jesus for you.

1 THESSALONIANS 5:16-18

Make a joyful shout unto the LORD all you lands! Serve the LORD with gladness. Come before His presence with singing.

PSALM 100:1–2

Give to the LORD the glory due His name; bring an offering, and come before him. Oh, worship the LORD in beauty of holiness!

1 CHRONICLES 16:29

Oh come, let us worship and bow down; Let us kneel before the LORD our Maker.

PSALM 95:6

AN ATMOSPHERE OF PRAISE

The memory came back to me just recently. Now that I think about it, it seems remarkable. But when I was growing up, it didn't seem remarkable at all.

Every time I ever saw my daddy take a drink of water, he paused to thank the Lord. He would fill a glass and then say, "I want to thank You for this water, in Jesus' name, Amen."

Daddy was one who took 1 Thessalonians 5:18 very literally. "In everything give thanks; for this is the will of God in Christ Jesus for you." Over the years I have become convinced that praise sets up a mantle of protection around the people of the Lord. Praise is an atmosphere through which the Adversary cannot move.

If you and I really entered into this truth, it would transform our lives. And it's not simply because praise can insulate or protect us. It's more than that. It's because *He is worthy* . . . worthy of the best of our praise, the depths of our thanksgiving.

Jack Hayford
Moments with Majesty

PRAYER

Be anxious for nothing, but in everything by prayer and supplication, with thanksgiving, let your requests be made known to God; and "The peace of God, which surpasses all understanding, will guard your hearts and minds through Christ Jesus."

PHILIPPIANS 4:6-7

For this cause everyone who is godly shall pray to You in a time when You may be found.

PSALM 32:6

If My people who are called by My name will humble themselves, and pray and seek My face, and turn from their wicked ways, then I will hear from heaven, and will forgive their sin and heal their land.

2 CHRONICLES 7:14

GIVE GOD YOUR WHISPERING THOUGHTS

Imagine considering every moment as a potential time of communion with God. By the time your life is over, you will have spent six months at stoplights, eight months opening junk mail, a year and a half looking for lost stuff (double that number in my case), and a whopping five years standing in various lines. Why don't you give these moments to God? By giving God your whispering thoughts, the common becomes uncommon. Simple phrases such as "Thank you, Father," "Be sovereign in this hour, O Lord," "You are my resting place, Jesus" can turn a commute into a pilgrimage. You needn't leave your office. . . . Just pray where you are. . . . Give God your whispering thoughts.

Max Lucado
Just Like Jesus

PRAYER

I say to you that if two of you agree on earth concerning anything that they ask, it will be done for them by My Father in heaven.

MATTHEW 18:19

Praying always with all prayer and supplication in the Spirit, being watchful to this end with all perseverance, and supplication for all the saints.

EPHESIANS 6:18

Brethren, pray for us, that the word of the Lord may run swiftly and be glorified.

2 THESSALONIANS 3:1

PRAYER IS A GIFT OF GRACE

Prayer is not a reward we deserve but a *privilege* given by God. It is His gift to us, not our gift to Him. No one is good enough to earn the ear of God. Prayer is a gift of His grace. The only requirement is the Father-child relationship given to all who have received Christ by faith (John 1:12).

There is no doubt about God's unwavering love for His children. He wants to hear from us not because we are deserving, but because it simply pleases Him to do so. To attempt to earn God's ear or refuse to come because of sin is to miss the entire point of grace. Both of these responses stem from pride. Our Father calls us to believe and consent to be loved, heard, and answered even though totally unworthy of that great position.

William Carr Peel
What God Does When Men Pray

PRAYER

Hear a just cause, O LORD, attend to my cry; give ear to my prayer which is not from deceitful lips.

PSALM 17:1

For the eyes of the Lord are on the righteous. And His ears are open to their prayers; but the face of the Lord is against those who do evil.

1 PETER 3:12

Hear me when I call O God of my righteousness! You have relieved me in my distress; Have mercy on me, and hear my prayer.

PSALM 4:1

The LORD has heard my supplication; The LORD will receive my prayer.

PSALM 6:9

THE BRIDGE OF CONFESSION

Here's a good rule of thumb: Those who keep secrets from God keep their distance from God. Those who are honest with God draw near to God. . . .

Secrets erect a fence while confession builds a bridge.

Once there were a couple of farmers who couldn't get along with each other. A wide ravine separated their two farms, but as a sign of their mutual distaste for each other, each constructed a fence on his side of the chasm to keep the other out.

In time, however, the daughter of one met the son of the other, and the couple fell in love. Determined not to be kept apart by the folly of their fathers, they tore down the fence and used the wood to build a bridge across the ravine.

Confession does that. Confessed sin becomes the bridge over which we can walk back into the presence of God.

Max Lucado
In the Grip of Grace

OBEYING GOD'S WORD

The word of the LORD is proven;
He is a shield to all who trust in Him.

PSALM 18:30

Whatever things were written before were
written for our learning, that we through
the patience and comfort of the Scriptures
might have hope.

ROMANS 15:4

Oh, that they had such a heart in them
that they would fear Me and always keep
all My commandments, that it might be
well with them and with their children
forever!

DEUTERONOMY 5:29

HUNGRY FOR GOD'S WORD

In my desire for a deep, abiding relationship with Jesus, I yearned after a deeper familiarity with God's Word. The only time for a few minutes in the Word was first thing in the morning. That's when I read the sports page. Months of brushing off the Word of God so I could read the sports page left me empty, miserable. . . .

I began to pray, "Please increase my love for Your Word more than anything else, *including* sports.". . . After many frustrating starts, I made a promise to myself and to God that I would refuse to read the newspaper until I'd spent meaningful time in the Word. . . .

Within a short time my appetite for the Word began to grow. My appreciation and love for Scripture soon dwarfed any appeal the sports page once held. And as my hunger and discipline for God and His Word continued to grow, God's power in my life grew proportionately.

Bill McCartney
Sold Out

OBEYING GOD'S WORD

The word of God is living and powerful, and sharper than any two-edged sword, piercing even to the division of soul and spirit, and of joints and marrow, and is a discerner of the thoughts and intents of the heart.

HEBREWS 4:12

As newborn babes, desire the pure milk of the word, that you may grow thereby.

1 PETER 2:2

*Oh, how I love Your law!
It is my meditation all the day.*

PSALM 119:97

A HEART FOR READING GOD'S WORD

The most basic aspect of spending time in the Scriptures is to simply read them. This is reading as you would read a novel, or a book from a Christian bookstore. It's reading for education, enlightenment, and enjoyment. This is the part of the journey where we allow God to speak to us ever so quietly through His Word. . . .

For many men, this kind of reading is the key part of the important daily routine called a *quiet time*.

When we read the Bible, we're listening to God speak to us. Thus, it's a wonderful idea to do it consistently.

E. Glenn Wagner
The Heart of a Godly Man

OBEYING GOD'S WORD

*The law of the L*ORD *is perfect,*
*   converting the soul;*
*The testimony of the L*ORD *is sure,*
*   making wise the simple;*
*The statutes of the L*ORD *are right,*
*   rejoicing the heart;*
*The commandment of the L*ORD *is pure,*
*   enlightening the eyes.*

PSALM 19:7–8

I understand more than the ancients,
Because I keep Your precepts.
I have restrained my feet from
*   every evil way,*
That I may keep Your word.

PSALM 119:100–101

GETTING A HANDLE ON GOD'S WORD

Over time you will learn that there are a variety of "delivery systems" for God's Word. At times you will simply *hear* the Word as someone like your pastor speaks on Sunday. At times you might *read* through large sections of the Bible as you would an exciting novel. As you being to grow you will probably find yourself wanting to understand the Bible at a more significant level, so you will begin to *study* it like a textbook. Your study might become so exciting that you find a verse or a passage that you want to *memorize*. . . . When God begins to speak to you through the Bible you will find yourself stopping to contemplate and reflect on what you are hearing. This is the practice of biblical *meditation*. These five delivery systems will help you get a handle on God's Word.

Dr. Bob Beltz
Daily Disciplines for the Christian Man

OBEYING GOD'S WORD

You are worthy, O Lord,
To receive glory and honor and power;
For You created all things,
And by Your will they exist and
*   were created.*

REVELATION 4:11

You shall observe My judgments and keep
My ordinances, to walk in them: I am the
LORD your God.

LEVITICUS 18:4

Draw near to God and He will draw near
to you.

JAMES 4:8

MAN'S ULTIMATE AIM

Our culture floods us with lies. The very word *advertisement* means to "advert," to lure away our attention by means of attractive—and often deceptive—claims. It isn't true that if you use a certain brand of toothpaste you will be cruising the Caribbean in a beautiful yacht. It isn't true that you can sleep around with multiple partners and enjoy a "good life." It isn't true that you can walk around sipping a cool drink from morning to night and stay sober, build healthy relationships, and find satisfaction in life. . . . It isn't true that you can relegate your faith to the corners of your life and be a satisfied, fulfilled, productive person.

Man's ultimate aim is to glorify God . . . period. There is no plan B. There is no viable alternative to exchanging my life for what God has declared to be important. . . . I glorify God by obeying Him, by doing that which is pleasing to Him.

Joseph C. Aldrich
Love for All Your Worth

DISCIPLINED SPIRITUALITY

You who love the Lʏᴏᴀ, hate evil!
He preserves the souls of His saints;
He delivers them out of the hand
*   of the wicked.*

PSALM 97:10

I can do all things through Christ
who strengthens me.

PHILIPPIANS 4:13

As for me, I will see Your face in
*   righteousness;*
I shall be satisfied when I awake in
*   Your likeness.*

PSALM 17:15

DWELLING IN GOD'S PRESENCE

Study and meditation on the Word [of God] was my lifeblood. It was my daily fuel for living. Trying to handle the scope and intensity of my daily obligations, however, rarely afforded me the restful times of simply dwelling in God's presence that I craved and needed. During the season, I would grab them when I could. . . . When I'd go before the Lord, I'd often leave feeling guilty that my prayers weren't more focused. . . . It was a tension I would battle the duration of my career—how to carve out the uninterrupted time I needed with the Lord when the demands of the football season were buzzing about me like angry hornets. Thankfully, I was still feeding on God's Word, disciplining myself, fasting, and centering myself in prayer.

Bill McCartney
Sold Out

DISCIPLINED SPIRITUALITY

His divine power has given to us all things that pertain to life and godliness, through the knowledge of Him who called us by glory and virtue, by which have been given to us exceedingly great and precious promises, that through these you may be partakers of the divine nature, having escaped the corruption that is in the world through lust.

2 PETER 1:3–4

It is God who works in you both to will and to do for His good pleasure.

PHILIPPIANS 2:13

*Blessed are those who keep His
     testimonies,
Who seek Him with the whole heart!*

PSALM 119:2

THE MIRACLE OF THE CHRISTIAN LIFE

Christ *in* me is the source of power that makes the Christian life possible. Only one person in all of human history has ever lived the Christian life. His name was Jesus. Only one person in all of history still has the ability to live the Christian life. His name is still Jesus. The miracle of the Christian life is found in the amazing and miraculous fact that Jesus Christ chooses to live His life through us! He has come to indwell my being and work in and *through* my personality. I can't, but He can! This is the secret of living an effective and fruitful spiritual life.

Dr. Bob Beltz
Daily Disciplines for the Christian Man

DISCIPLINED SPIRITUALITY

"Let him who glories glory in this,
That he understands and knows Me,
That I am the LORD, exercising loving
*   kindness, judgment, and righteousness*
*   in the earth.*
For in these I delight," says the LORD.

JEREMIAH 9:24

We do not have a High Priest who cannot
sympathize with our weaknesses, but was
in all points tempted as we are, yet with-
out sin.

HEBREWS 4:15

Be sober, be vigilant; because your adver-
sary the devil walks about like a roaring
lion, seeking whom he may devour.

1 PETER 5:8

CHARACTER MATTERS

The word *character* comes from the word *cut* or *etch*. It is the picture of a sharp instrument in the hands of an artist who is taking a blank canvas and beginning to cut grooves until an image appears.

Not far from my hometown of Fayetteville, Arkansas is . . . Silver Dollar City. I have three young kids at home and we still go at least once a year. On one of my early trips, I went to the front gate of the park and came into contact with a couple of Ozark mountain men in overalls doing woodwork. They took a big block of wood and began to cut grooves in it. My kids pulled me off to other sights in the park, but on the way out that evening I stopped back by the mountain men to see what kind of progress they had made. I looked down and from that big block of wood they had carved the head of a bear. It was incredible!

What does this mean to us? Every decision we make, every choice we make, every day, is a cut and a groove in the picture of our character. . . . Character matters.

Stephen Graves
(speech, Birmingham, Alabama, 1997)

DISCIPLINED SPIRITUALITY

My flesh and my heart fail;
But God is the strength of my heart
and my portion forever.

PSALM 73:26

And He said to me, "My grace is sufficient
for you, for My strength is made perfect in
weakness. Therefore most gladly I will
rather boast in my infirmities, that the
power of Christ may rest upon me."

2 CORINTHIANS 12:9

Those who wait on the LORD
Shall renew their strength;
They shall mount up with wings
like eagles,
They shall run and not be weary,
They shall walk and not faint.

ISAIAH 40:31

SAYING YES TO WHAT IS RIGHT

It's obvious that if you are not exercising your-self spiritually, you're not going to be in great spiritual shape. Many of us will give an hour a day to exercise and sweat for our bodies, but we aren't willing to sweat for the kingdom.

The first time kingdom work puts a little bead of sweat on our foreheads, we say, "Christianity is too hard." Of course it is hard. It wasn't sup-posed to be easy.

But let me tell you, if you sweat long enough and regularly enough, you'll have spiritual energy you didn't have before. . . .

But this takes discipline. It means saying *yes* to what is right and *no* to what is wrong.

Tony Evans
What a Way to Live!

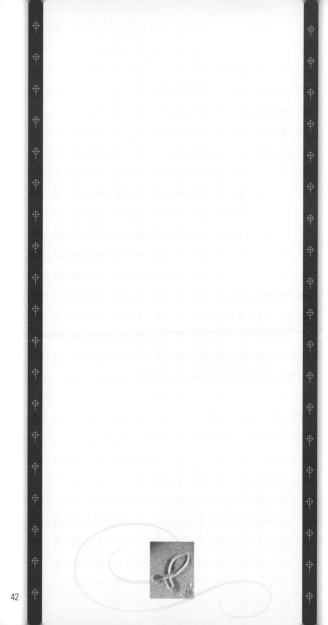

A MAN AND HIS FRIENDS

FRIENDSHIP WITH CHRISTIAN BROTHERS

*A man who has friends must himself
be friendly,
But there is a friend who sticks closer
than a brother.*

PROVERBS 18:24

*Two are better than one,
Because they have a good reward for
their labor.
For if they fall, one will lift up his
companion.
But woe to him who is alone when he falls,
For he has no one to help him up.*

ECCLESIASTES 4:9–10

*Be kindly affectionate to one another with
brotherly love, in honor giving preference
to one another.*

ROMANS 12:10

THE SHELTERING TREE OF FRIENDSHIP

The poet Samuel Coleridge once described friendship as "a sheltering tree." When you have this quality, the branches of your friendship reach out over the lives of others, giving them shelter, shade, rest, relief, and encouragement. . . .

Friends give comfort. We find strength near them. . . . When something troublesome occurs in our life, we pick up the phone and call a friend, needing the comfort he . . . provides. Friends also care enough about us to hold us accountable . . . but we never doubt their love or respect. . . .

The flip side of that is equally healthy—our being friends like that to others. It works both ways.

Charles R. Swindoll
Hope Again

FRIENDSHIP WITH
CHRISTIAN BROTHERS

A friend loves at all times
And a brother is born for adversity.

PROVERBS 17:17

As iron sharpens iron,
So a man sharpens the countenance
of his friend.

PROVERBS 27:17

Confess your trespasses to one another,
and pray for one another, that you may be
healed. The effective, fervent prayer of a
righteous man avails much.

JAMES 5:16

GOD WITH SKIN ON

You and I need each other to be as sharp as God intends us to be, living on the very cutting edge of the mission He's given us.

The beasts and birds of the field and the air know this. Did you know the reason geese fly in a flock? It's because they have a serious, hard, difficult mission—to cross a continent. Wildlife biologists tell us that by flying together, they increase their range 71 percent.

Jesus sent his men on missions two by two. He never sent his men alone. Now, when I'm in pain and have lost my perspective, I can manage not to read the Bible. . . . I can quench the Spirit of God. But when my brother is standing with me—God with skin on—I can't get away from him. He's there for me. He is my Jonathan. You and I need that. As iron sharpens iron, so one man sharpens another.

Stu Weber
(speech, Birmingham, Alabama, 1997)

FRIENDSHIP WITH
CHRISTIAN BROTHERS

And if one member suffers, all the members suffer with it; or if one member is honored, all the members rejoice with it.

1 CORINTHIANS 12:26

For as the body is one and has many members, but all the members of that one body, being many are one body, so also is Christ. For by one Spirit we were all baptized into one body.

1 CORINTHIANS 13:12

Abide in Me and I in you. As the branch cannot bear fruit of itself, unless it abides in the vine, neither can you, unless you abide in Me. I am the vine, you are the branches. He who abides in Me and I in him bears much fruit; for without Me you can do nothing.

JOHN 15:4–5

STONES IN THE SAME BUILDING

A Presbyterian believer and a Baptist believer are joined to the same vine, they're engaged to the same Lord, they're in the same sheepfold, they're stones in the same building, they're indwelt by the same Spirit. They probably even study the same Book and sing the same hymns. . . .

The imagery is not of one vine nourishing just one branch. The life of God flows to myriad branches. God has no "only child."

There's a second joining. The first is vertical between man and God. The second is horizontal between man and man. Through the baptism of the Spirit, all believers are joined to the Body of Christ.

Joe Aldrich
Reunitus

FRIENDSHIP WITH
CHRISTIAN BROTHERS

Since you have purified your souls in obeying the truth through the Spirit in sincere love of the brethren, love one another fervently with a pure heart.

1 PETER 1:22

A new commandment I give to you, that you love one another; as I have loved you, that you also love one another.

JOHN 13:34

Therefore be imitators of God as dear children. And walk in love, as Christ also has loved us and given Himself for us, an offering and a sacrifice to God for a sweet-smelling aroma.

EPHESIANS 5:1-2

YOU BELONG TO A TEAM

We live in a culture that encourages independence and self-reliance, but the facts speak for themselves. Giving one's mind, talent, and energy to a team beats anything we can do by ourselves. "Two are better than one" (Eccles. 4:9). Joining together with another multiplies our joy, brings out the best in us, and raises our commitment level. But teams aren't just for sports. Far from it. The fact is, you, too, belong to a team—or teams. In your daily life, wherever you're linked with others in pursuit of a shared goal or belief, that's your team.

Bill McCartney
Sold Out

ACCOUNTABILITY TO CHRISTIAN BROTHERS

Confess your trespasses to one another, and pray for one another, that you may be healed. The effective, fervent prayer of a righteous man avails much.

JAMES 5:16

Everyone helped his neighbor, and said to his brother, "Be of good courage!"

ISAIAH 41:6

Whoever does the will of My father in heaven is my brother and sister and mother.

MATTHEW 12:50

NO LONE-RANGER CHRISTIANS

One of the problems we men in the church have is that too many of us are "Lone-Ranger" Christians. We're trying to make it all by ourselves. But I would remind you that even the Lone Ranger had a partner.

When you feel like you aren't going to make it as a dad or as a husband or when the job is dragging you down, you need some brothers to come alongside, hold up your hands, and say, "We're going to make it together, brother. We're going to hang in there with you. We're going to prevail for God."

As you grow in the Lord, you will also be able to hold up another man's hands when he is tired. That's the ministry of the body of Christ in action.

Tony Evans
What a Way to Live!

ACCOUNTABILITY TO
CHRISTIAN BROTHERS

Let each of you look out not only for his own interests, but also for the interests of others.

PHILIPPIANS 2:4

By this all will know that you are My disciples, if you have love for one another.

JOHN 13:35

Walk worthy of the calling with which you were called, with all lowliness and gentleness, with longsuffering, bearing with one another in love, endeavoring to keep the unity of the Spirit in the bond of peace.

EPHESIANS 4:1–3

A COVENANT RELATIONSHIP

I really believe in the meaning that lies behind the term *accountability*. The term itself, I don't care for. . . .

I have a description that works better for me than *accountability*. I like using the term *covenant relationship*. The main thing I like about it is that it highlights the fact that every person in the relationship has responsibilities. . . . What are the essential elements of a covenant relationship?

Trust: I trust you and you trust me. . . .

Commitment: You won't leave me when I mess up. . . .

Honesty: You'll tell me what I need to hear, not just what I want to hear.

E. Glenn Wagner
The Heart of a Godly Man

ACCOUNTABILITY TO
CHRISTIAN BROTHERS

If we confess our sins, he is faithful and just to forgive us our sins and to cleanse us from all unrighteousness.

1 JOHN 1:9

Brethren, if anyone among you wanders from the truth, and someone turns him back, let him know that he who turns a sinner from the error of his way will save a soul from death and cover a multitude of sins.

JAMES 5:19–20

Now you are the body of Christ, and members individually.

1 CORINTHIANS 12:27

EVERY MAN NEEDS A FRIEND

I believe that if Jonathan had lived, David would never have experienced the Bathsheba episode in his life.

Those two men knew one another. Their souls were wrapped around one another.

I believe that if Jonathan had lived, he would have seen the strange things happening in his friend's life. He would have seen the light go out of David's eyes. He would have seen the lethargy slip into his life, and he would have said, "David, it's springtime, remember? This is the time we go to battle. Let's you and I go."

Do you have a friend like that? Every man needs a man for a friend. I honestly believe that the pathway to godliness wanders straight through the door of masculine friendship.

Stu Weber
(speech, Buffalo, New York, 1997)

ACCOUNTABILITY TO CHRISTIAN BROTHERS

The ear that hears the rebukes of life
Will abide among the wise.
He who disdains instruction despises
* his own soul,*
But he who heeds rebuke gets
* understanding.*

PROVERBS 15:31–32

Brethren, if a man is overtaken in any
trespass, you who are spiritual restore such
a one in a spirit of gentleness, considering
yourself lest you also be tempted.

GALATIANS 6:1

And let us consider one another in order to
stir up love and good works.

HEBREWS 10:24

HELPING EACH OTHER TO
RUN THE RACE

Dr. Fong tells a great story about nine kids who had trained for many months for a Special Olympic race. The gun went off, and these nine kids took off. At the first corner, one fell down, scraped his leg, and screamed in pain. A few seconds later, he let out another scream of anguish when he realized that he would never be able to finish the race.

Then an amazing thing happened. The other eight kids stopped and walked back to him. They knelt down, put their arms around him, and brushed off his face. One girl bent down and kissed his knee, and they slowly helped him up.

Together arm in arm, all nine of those precious kids walked across the finish line together.

My friends, when you fall in the race of life—and it is not *if*, it's *when*—do you have others who will stop and come back and put their arms around you and help you across that line?

Gary Oliver
(speech, Chicago, Illinois, 1997)

ACCOUNTABILITY TO
CHRISTIAN BROTHERS

Therefore be imitators of God as dear children. And walk in love, as Christ also has loved us and given Himself for us, an offering and a sacrifice to God for a sweet-smelling aroma.

EPHESIANS 5:1–2

He who covers a transgression seeks love, But he who repeats a matter separates friends.

PROVERBS 17:9

All of you be of one mind, having compassion for one another, love as brothers, be tenderhearted, be courteous; not returning evil for evil or reviling for reviling, but on the contrary blessing, knowing that you were called to this, that you may inherit a blessing.

1 PETER 3:8–9

SHARED GOALS

When we share our goals with others, whether with family members or friends, we become increasingly motivated to attain these goals because we know we will be held accountable. There is a great deal of discomfort associated with knowing that we have not attained our goals, and that others we care about know this, too. This feeling of accountability, when coupled with support, is a tremendous motivating factor.

When we get discouraged or disappointed that we haven't progressed as far as we would like, the support of our family and friends can generate energy within us. This energy drives us to go forward, even when many times it seems easier to give up. Just having someone say, "How are you doing?" or "You can do it," is tremendously energizing.

Gary Smalley
The Key to Your Child's Heart

A MAN AND HIS INTEGRITY

SEXUAL PURITY

If you live according to the flesh you will die; but if by the Spirit you put to death the deeds of the body, you will live. For as many as are led by the Spirit of God, these are sons of God.

ROMANS 8:13–14

Blessed are the pure in heart, for they shall see God.

MATTHEW 5:8

For the weapons of our warfare are not carnal but mighty in God for pulling down strongholds, casting down arguments and every high thing that exalts itself against the knowledge of God, bringing every thought into captivity to the obedience of Christ.

2 CORINTHIANS 10:4-5

TEMPTED TO LINGER

As David found when he was tempted by the bathing Bathsheba, the initial enticement is rarely to sin. It's more often a temptation to linger too long. And that becomes the first link in a chain of seemingly innocent choices that lead to destruction. From the clear teaching of Scripture, from my own experience, and from the stories of thousands of other men, I can tell you that *the longer you linger, the sooner you'll stumble.* Godly men are prompt to do God's will.

If we don't *immediately* identify tempting thoughts and take them captive to what we know to be true—if we don't *immediately* replace the wrong thinking with right thinking—we'll become so weak that we won't care what we do until *after* we've sinned and begun to taste the bitter consequences.

Gary J. Oliver
Go the Distance

SEXUAL PURITY

Blessed are those who keep justice,
And he who does righteousness at
*   all times!*

PSALM 106:3

What does the LORD your God require of
you, but to fear the LORD your God, to
walk in all His ways and to love Him, to
serve the LORD your God with all your
heart and with all your soul, and to keep
the commandments of the LORD and His
statutes which I command you today for
your good?

DEUTERONOMY 10:12-13

A righteous man who falters before the
wicked is like a murky spring and a
polluted well.

PROVERBS 25:26

IMMORALITY: THE MORTAL ENEMY

Henry Ford found success in the car industry by mass producing his Model T automobile. When he and his wife Clara reached their fiftieth wedding anniversary in 1938, Ford was asked the secret of his long marriage. He responded, "The formula is the same as I used to make a successful car. Stick to one model."

If we plan to stick to one model, then we have to flee all the others. We must run from any threat to sexual purity.

It's a fail-proof strategy for avoiding sexual sin. Yet that should be no surprise, because it comes directly from God himself. . . . He knows that the power of immoral sex can destroy us if we don't treat it like a mortal enemy.

Steve Farrar
Point Man

SEXUAL PURITY

I have been crucified with Christ; it is no longer I who live, but Christ lives in me; and the life which I now live in the flesh I live by faith in the Son of God, who loved me and gave Himself for me.

GALATIANS 2:20

Flee sexual immorality. Every sin that a man does is outside the body, but he who commits sexual immorality sins against his own body. Or do you not know that your body is the temple of the Holy Spirit who is in you, whom you have from God, and you are not your own? For you were bought at a price; therefore glorify God in your body and in your spirit, which are God's.

1 CORINTHIANS 6:18–20

A TEMPLE OF THE HOLY SPIRIT

If a man wants to experience the power and grace of God, if he wants to see the Holy Spirit work, there is no more powerful arena for this than in his sexual life.

Our sexuality hits the very core of who we are. Much of the validation that women get in friendships, men get from the sexual relationship. Much of our identity and ego is at stake. . . .

We men have an incredible ability—a disability, really—to disassociate one area of our lives from another and justify wrong behavior that we would find unacceptable in others. . . .

Yet in 1 Corinthians 6:18–20, God . . . calls us to a higher standard. We're to honor Him with our bodies because they are a temple of the Holy Spirit, bought at the price of God's own Son. . . . That's a high standard, indeed.

Gregg Lewis
The Power of a Promise Kept

SEXUAL PURITY

My son, give me your heart,
And let your eyes observe my ways.
For a harlot is a deep pit,
And a seductress is a narrow well.

PROVERBS 23:26–27

With my whole heart I have sought You;
Oh, let me not wander from your
    commandments!
Your word I have hidden in my heart,
That I might not sin against you.

PSALM 119:10–11

My little children, these things I write to
you, so that you may not sin. And if any-
one sins, we have an Advocate with the
Father, Jesus Christ the righteous.

1 JOHN 2:1

SEXUAL PURITY MATTERS TO GOD

Choosing to let Jesus be Lord of your sex life will shape *every* other area of your life, because sexuality is at the center of our being. This decision will influence your current and future ability as a husband, father, and Christian. Choosing purity is difficult, but for those who put in the hard work and prayer, living by Christ's standard is a road to deep joy and *real* sexual satisfaction. At no time in history has our society been more in need of men willing to stand up, be different, and demonstrate the joy of living by a fundamentally better standard.

Purity, in its essence, is a reflection of God's character and presence in our lives. To the extent that we live in sexual purity, we reflect for the whole world that God is at work within us, shaping our desires, choices, and actions with more than just hormones.

Jerry Kirk
Seven Promises of a Promise Keeper

MORAL CONDUCT

My son, if your heart is wise, My heart will rejoice—indeed, I myself; yes, my inmost being will rejoice when your lips speak right things.

PROVERBS 23:16

If any of you lacks wisdom, let him ask of God, who gives to all liberally and without reproach, and it will be given to him. But let him ask in faith, with no doubting, for he who doubts is like a wave of the sea driven and tossed by the wind. For let not that man suppose that he will receive anything from the Lord; he is a double-minded man, unstable in all his ways.

JAMES 1:5–8

To be carnally minded is death, but to be spiritually minded is life and peace.

ROMANS 8:6

OUR WORD IS OUR BOND

I remember from my youth when men's character was much stronger and richer in integrity. The moral climate was such that lying, cheating, and stealing were gross sins. Those caught in them were dismissed from school, barred from practicing law, voted out of public office, and ruined in reputation. When a man gave you his word and shook your hand, it was better than a signed contract; it was a covenant. . . .

Such is not the rule today. Lawyers draw up legal papers with infinite pains to cover every detail of the agreement. . . . Even in marriage, men still vow to remain wed "until death do us part," but too often they treat their vow as part of a ritual without true meaning. . . .

When men don't hold to a high value of truth, they don't place a high value on their word, either.

Edwin Louis Cole
Seven Promises of a Promise Keeper

MORAL CONDUCT

Finally, brethren, whatever things are true, whatever things are noble, whatever things are just, whatever things are pure, whatever things are lovely, whatever things are of good report, if there is any virtue and if there is anything praiseworthy—meditate on these things.

PHILIPPIANS 4:8

Happy is the man who finds wisdom, and the man who gains understanding; for her proceeds are better than the profits of silver, and her gain than fine gold.

PROVERBS 3:13–14

Being confident of this very thing, that He who has begun a good work in you will complete it until the day of Jesus Christ.

PHILIPPIANS 1:6

MORE THAN GOOD INTENTIONS

Most Christian men want to be strong and victorious. We want to hear God say, "Well done, thou good and faithful servant." We want our lives to be characterized by integrity. The problem is that each of us has blind spots, weaknesses, and deeply entrenched habits that can sabotage our best intentions.

We need to move beyond biblical absolute and determine what kinds of things are healthy for us and what kinds are unhealthy. What one man can watch or listen to with no problem may open the door to unnecessary temptation for another man and increase his vulnerability to sin. . . .

Moral failure is rarely the result of a blowout; almost always, it's the result of a slow leak.

Gary J. Oliver
Seven Promises of a Promise Keeper

MORAL CONDUCT

He who has clean hands and a pure heart,
Who has not lifted up his soul to an idol,
Nor sworn deceitfully.
He shall receive blessing from the LORD,
And righteousness from the God of
his salvation.

PSALM 24:4–5

But the fruit of the Spirit is love, joy,
peace, longsuffering, kindness, goodness,
faithfulness, gentleness, self-control.
Against such there is no law. And those
who are Christ's have crucified the flesh
with its passions and desires. If we live in
the Spirit, let us also walk in the Spirit.

GALATIANS 5:22–25

ALIGNED WITH GOD'S PURPOSE

Few characters in the Bible evoke as much consternation as Samson. His recurring failure lay in his inability to align his life with the purpose for which God had formed him. . . .

Samson could never tame his passions and bring them under the control of his greater call. He faltered when he fell in love with a Philistine woman . . . stumbled . . . when he was lured into the bed of a prostitute . . . and wrecked himself when Delilah toyed with him until he betrayed his sacred trust before God. He audaciously believed that he still had the strength God had given to him. Instead, his enemies humiliated him. . . . All this because he had lost sight of God's purpose for his life. . . .

The places we go, the friendships we embrace, the language we use, the shows we watch, the books we read, the thoughts we entertain—all must be aligned with the purpose to which we are called by God.

Ravi Zacharias
Cries of the Heart

MORAL CONDUCT

The LORD will guide you continually,
And satisfy your soul in drought,
And strengthen our bones;
You shall be like a watered garden.
And like a spring of water whose waters
*   do not fail.*

ISAIAH 58:11

You will show me the path of life;
In Your presence is fullness of joy;
At Your right hand are pleasures
*   forevermore.*

PSALM 16:11

You are of God, little children, and have
overcome them, because He who is in you
is greater than he who is in the world.

1 JOHN 4:4

A SIMPLE LITTLE PRAYER

If we are going to be God's men, we need to live a lifestyle of repentance. As soon as we are conscious that we have gotten off the track, we need to change our course. One of the classics of Christian spirituality is a book written by a Russian monk entitled *The Way of the Pilgrim*. In this book, the monk talks about the use of what has become known as the Jesus Prayer. It is a simple little prayer that says, "Lord Jesus Christ, have mercy on me, a sinner." This little prayer (or one very similar to it) will probably be uttered repeatedly by the man who wants to walk with Christ. It is a prayer of repentance.

Bob Beltz
Daily Disciplines for the Christian Man

ETHICAL PRINCIPLES

Depart from evil, and do good;
And dwell forevermore.
*For the L*ORD *loves justice,*
And does not forsake His saints.

PSALM 37:27–28

*Blessed is the man who fears the L*ORD,
Who delights greatly in His
commandments.

PSALM 112:1

Walk in wisdom toward those who are
outside, redeeming the time. Let your
speech always be with grace, seasoned
with salt, that you may know how you
ought to answer each one.

COLOSSIANS 4:5–6

A PROMISE MADE, A PROMISE KEPT

The ability to make and keep promises is central to manhood. It may be trite to say that "a man's word is his bond," but it is never trite to see it in action. It is a man at his best—giving his word and making good on it, making a promise and keeping it. The calling of every man is to offer stability to a world full of chaos. Certainty to a jungle of unpredictability. Consistency to a world in flux. Security to an insecure place.

We live in a "hope so" world. There are few certainties in this life. Ours is a world of dreams, hopes, and wishful thinking. . . .

Everyone would love to change their hope to certainty. And we can, in the things that matter. The things inside. A real man brings certainty to his world by the power of a promise. . . . Promise making and keeping is at the heart of godliness.

Stu Weber
Tender Warrior

ETHICAL PRINCIPLES

But you, O man of God, . . . pursue righteousness, godliness, faith, love, patience, gentleness. Fight the good fight of faith, lay hold on eternal life. . . .

1 TIMOTHY 6:11–12

Beloved, let us cleanse ourselves from all filthiness of the flesh and spirit, perfecting holiness in the fear of God.

2 CORINTHIANS 7:1

Teach me O L<small>ORD</small>, the way of Your statutes, and I shall keep it to the end. Give me understanding, and I shall keep Your law; indeed, I shall observe it with my whole heart.

PSALM 119:33–34

A REFLECTION OF WHAT'S INSIDE

Integrity means that what's on the outside is a reflection of what's inside; it's the real substance of a man. Daniel illustrates this quality beautifully. When an order went forth that people were only allowed to pray in the name of Babylon's King Darius (Daniel 6), Daniel went to his upstairs room, where the windows were open, got down on his knees, and prayed to the God of heaven three times a day—"as he had been doing previously" (Daniel 6:10 NASB). There was no false show, but rather the simple living out of what was on the inside. It's interesting to note that not one negative thing is said about him in Scripture.

E. Glenn Wagner
The Heart of a Godly Man

ETHICAL PRINCIPLES

My brethren, be strong in the Lord and in the power of His might. Put on the whole armor of God, that you may be able to stand against the wiles of the devil.

EPHESIANS 6:10–11

Walk in the Spirit, and you shall not fulfill the lust of the flesh.

GALATIANS 5:16

Most assuredly, I say to you, whoever commits sin is a slave of sin. And a slave does not abide in the house forever, but a son abides forever. Therefore if the Son makes you free, you shall be free indeed.

JOHN 8:34–36

FOCUS YOUR THOUGHTS ON CHRIST

I'm convinced that the battle with this world is a battle within the mind. Our minds are major targets of the Enemy's appeal. When the world pulls back its bowstring, our minds are the bull's-eyes. Any arrows we allow to become impaled in our minds will ultimately poison our thoughts. And if we tolerate this long enough, we'll end up acting out what we think. A technique for counteracting that poison, for dealing with the seduction of the world around us, is to focus our minds on Christ. We can do this by remembering what our Savior has done for us.

Charles R. Swindoll
Hope Again

A MAN AND HIS FAMILY

COMMITTED TO YOUR WIFE

He who finds a wife finds a good thing,
and obtains favor from the LORD.

PROVERBS 18:22

Many waters cannot quench love,
Nor can the floods drown it.

SONG OF SOLOMON 8:7

I want you to know that the head of
every man is Christ, the head of woman
is man, and the head of Christ is God.

1 CORINTHIANS 11:3

A LOVE THAT LASTS

From looking at my own marriage and hundreds of others, I've come to understand that enriching the life of another is often more satisfying than doing something for ourselves. As we reach out to another, our own needs for fulfillment and love are met.

I've seen that the most satisfied, joyous couples are those who have learned heroic love and practice it daily. When a husband and wife both want their partner to receive life's best before they do, you have a marriage that's going to exceed every wedding day dream. Their love not only lasts; it continually grows.

Gary Smalley
Making Love Last Forever

COMMITTED TO YOUR WIFE

Who can find a virtuous wife?
For her worth is far above rubies.
The heart of her husband safely trusts her;
So he will have no lack of gain.

PROVERBS 31:10–11

Let each man have his own wife, and let
each woman have her own husband. Let
the husband render to his wife the affec-
tion due her, and likewise also the wife to
her husband.

1 CORINTHIANS 7:2–3

Husbands ought to love their own wives as
their own bodies; he who loves his wife
loves himself. For no one ever hated his
own flesh, but nourishes and cherishes it,
just as the Lord does the church.

EPHESIANS 5:28–29

SAILING WITH YOUR FIRST MATE

To build a seaworthy marriage craft, men need more than relational skills. Christ must be Captain, Scripture the firm anchor, the Church a willing crew, and the marriage commitment a sound framework. That will hold us from the brink. We need practice paddling in calmer waters—to develop positive strokes, warm memories, and confidence in our boat.

Knowing how to rely on the Captain, the anchor, other crew members, and your partner will get you through troubled waters. The couple heading for dangerous waters or the false security of a pond needs the oars of faith for paddling upstream out of harm's way. Muscles of faith and hope to believe God for rougher, deeper waters must be exercised well *before* facing the challenge of whitewater rapids.

E. Glenn Wagner
Strategies for a Successful Marriage

COMMITTED TO YOUR WIFE

Husbands, love your wives and do not be bitter toward them.

COLOSSIANS 3:19

In all things showing yourself to be a pattern of good works; in doctrine showing integrity, reverence, incorruptibility.

TITUS 2:7

Houses and riches are an inheritance
*   from fathers,*
But a prudent wife is from the LORD.

PROVERBS 19:14

SUCCESS AT YOUR SECOND JOB

Biblical leadership means that when you come home, you come home to your second job. You don't come home to pick up the newspaper, you don't come home to pick up the TV channel surfer, you come home to dry the dishes as your wife washes them. You come home to help get the kids ready for bed.

Then you get down on your knees, beside the bed, you and your wife, and you dedicate your children to God. Biblical leadership means that your wife is not stifled; she grows, and blossoms, and flourishes, and she becomes significant because you love her, support her, encourage her, help her, affirm her, and strengthen her. It means you lay your hands on each one of your children and on your wife and you bless them in the name of God.

That's spiritual leadership.

Tony Evans
(speech before Promise Keepers)

COMMITTED TO YOUR WIFE

Let nothing be done through selfish ambition or conceit, but in lowliness of mind let each esteem others better than himself.

PHILIPPIANS 2:3

Love suffers long and is kind; love does not envy; love does not parade itself, is not puffed up; does not rejoice in iniquity, but rejoices in the truth; bears all things, believes all things, hopes all things, endures all things. Love never fails.

1 CORINTHIANS 13:4–8

The heart of the wise teaches his mouth,
And adds learning to his lips.
Pleasant words are like a honeycomb,
Sweetness to the soul and health to
    the bones.

PROVERBS 16:23–24

IT SOUNDS LIKE LOVE

Every romance, to become a deepening relationship, must come to the point of accepting responsibility for "setting up house." This involves accepting the commitment of marriage, assuming certain duties, and attending to certain details. Does this mean that you lose the electric thrill of the merely "romantic"? Perhaps. But you don't lose love. In fact, love is given a new dimension in which to mature. . . .

Romance is fine. Flowers and candles and goose bumps have their place. But it is *commitment* that binds the wounds, pays the bills, stands the heat, and hangs in there regardless of the cost.

The former sounds like a fling. The latter sounds like love.

Jack Hayford
Moments with Majesty

FAITHFUL TO YOUR WIFE

Charm is deceitful and beauty is passing,
But a woman who fears the LORD, she
shall be praised.

PROVERBS 31:30

This is the will of God, your sanctification:
that you should abstain from sexual
immorality; that each of you should know
how to possess his own vessel in sanctifica-
tion and honor, not in passion of lust, like
the Gentiles who do not know God.

1 THESSALONIANS 4:3–5

Marriage is honorable among all, and the
bed undefiled; but fornicators and adul-
terers God will judge.

HEBREWS 13:4

THE MYTH OF THE IDEAL MATE

Many men are perfectionists who place such high expectations upon their wives that they can never measure up. This ideal-mate syndrome is pictured in the commercials we watch. For once wouldn't it be nice to see a slightly overweight woman trying to sell you a car or after-shave lotion? . . .

Such made-for-the-male-fantasy images soon send us home to our less-than-perfect mate, saying, "My wife doesn't measure up." (Get real, guys, neither do you!) Is your wife a victim of unreasonable demands?

The Bible warns husbands about trapping our wives with such unreasonable demands. Instead, a husband is to live with his wife in an understanding or considerate way. . . . Such unreasonable demands only tear down your marriage. . . . Stop trying to change your wife. If you keep trying to change her, you'll drive the two of you crazy.

E. Glenn Wagner
Strategies for a Successful Marriage

FAITHFUL TO YOUR WIFE

From the beginning of the creation, God made them male and female. For this reason a man shall leave his father and mother and be joined to his wife, and the two shall become one flesh; so then they are no longer two, but one flesh. Therefore what God has joined together, let not man separate.

MARK 10:6–9

Delight yourself also in the LORD,
And he shall give you the desires
of your heart.
Commit your way to the LORD,
Trust also in Him,
And He shall bring it to pass.

PSALM 37:4–5

THE MOST BEAUTIFUL WOMAN
IN THE WORLD

The woman you chose to be your wife—that woman who attracted your attention with her beauty, her charm, her intelligence, and maybe even her ability to bake a mean German chocolate cake—must be to you the most beautiful woman in the world.

You must be able to say to her . . . "You are beautiful, my darling."

It must be a heartfelt expression. The pretty woman who shares your bed must be to you the epitome of loveliness. . . .

Every day, the woman you married must hear from your lips how beautiful she is. Every day, you must be able to thank God for her and praise His guidance that led the two of you together.

Steve Farrar
Point Man

FAITHFUL TO YOUR WIFE

No temptation has overtaken you except such as is common to man; but God is faithful, who will not allow you to be tempted beyond what you are able, but with the temptation will also make the way of escape, that you may be able to bear it.

1 CORINTHIANS 10:13

Let your fountain be blessed,
And rejoice with the wife of your youth.
As a loving deer and a graceful doe,
Let her breasts satisfy you at all times;
Always be enraptured with her love.

PROVERBS 5:18–19

MORALITY IS NOT A "DRIVE-THROUGH" ISSUE

Have you ever heard this argument? "Sex is no different than eating. You get hungry, you eat. You get turned on, you have sex. It's the same thing.". . .

For many people today, indulging their sexual desires has become as ordinary as eating when they are hungry. But Paul said in no uncertain terms that while the stomach is made for food, our bodies are not made for immorality [1 Cor. 6:13].

In other words, morality is not a "drive-through" issue. It is not the same as eating—or anything else, for that matter.

Why? Because our bodies were made for the Lord. . . . They are much more than a container for sexual desires. Our bodies are vehicles through which we are to honor and serve God and bring Him glory. What we do with our bodies impacts our spirits, and that impacts eternity.

Tony and Lois Evans
Seasons of Love

FAITHFUL TO YOUR WIFE

Your word I have hidden in my heart,
That I might not sin against You.

PSALM 119:11

If you will indeed obey My voice and keep
My covenant, then you shall be a special
treasure to me above all people.

EXODUS 19:5

Whatever you do in word or deed, do all
in the name of the Lord Jesus, giving
thanks to God the Father through Him.

COLOSSIAN 3:17

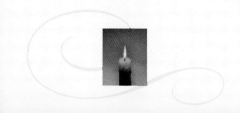

THE SEX TREE

A couple's sex life can be compared to an apple tree. If we nurture the tree and keep it healthy, we're going to have fruit on it. But if we neglect it and don't nurture it, it's not likely to bear much fruit. If we get impatient for fruit in the springtime, remembering the delicious taste of apples and complaining that we haven't had fruit lately, we might start picking the blossoms off. But they don't taste like fruit, and once you pick them off, you'll never get apples.

A healthy tree needs water, sunlight, air, and fertilized soil—it takes all four ingredients. Likewise, when we nurture a marriage verbally, emotionally, physically, and spiritually, we can watch the love and intimacy and knowledge grow. And as they develop, the marital tree will provide a steady supply of fruit. Then any time we want, basically, we can pick off the fruit and eat it, and it's delicious! Why? Because we've nurtured the sex tree—the relationship.

Gary Smalley
Making Love Last Foreve

HONORING YOUR WIFE

As the elect of God, holy and beloved, put on tender mercies, kindness, humility, meekness, longsuffering, bearing with one another, and forgiving one another, if anyone has a complaint against another; even as Christ forgave you, so you also must do.

COLOSSIANS 3:12

Do all things without complaining and disputing, that you may become blameless and harmless, children of God without fault in the midst of a crooked and perverse generation, among whom you shine as lights in the world.

PHILIPPIANS 2:14–15

THREE IMPERATIVES FOR HUSBANDS

So what are a woman's needs? What are the prerequisites for learning this wonderful, sometimes-bewildering language called "Woman"? Dr. Harley isolates five. The first is her need for *affection*, that is, tenderness. The second is *conversation*, the sharing of the heart. The third is *honesty* and *openness*; no secrets between us. The fourth is *security*, or physical and financial provision. The fifth is *relational commitment*. She must know she is a priority.

Scripture refines those five feminine needs down into three imperatives for men: *honor, nourish, cherish.*

And listen friends, that's no academic exercise—*it's an action plan.*

Stu Weber
Tender Warrior

HONORING YOUR WIFE

This I pray, that your love may abound still more and more in knowledge and all discernment.

PHILIPPIANS 1:9

Husbands, love your wives, just as Christ also loved the church and gave Himself for her.

EPHESIANS 5:25

Bear one another's burdens, and so fulfill the law of Christ.

GALATIANS 6:2

LOVING AND SERVING

Life was designed to be about love. Love is about relationships. If we are to build our life on the foundation of Christ and His Word, we need a working set of relationship priorities. The highest priority of life needs to be our relationship with Christ. . . .

For those of us who are married, our wives are to be the highest priority . . . next to Christ. This is where peacemaking needs to begin. Our homes are the laboratories God has designed to teach us to love and to serve. . . .

For those of us who have children, they are to be the next priority after our wives. If we are going to live in conformity with the divine design, we will need to work at giving the proper attention, time, and energy to loving and serving our children. . . . We need to be thinking that when we come home from work, we actually begin the most important work of our day.

Dr. Bob Beltz
Daily Disciplines for the Christian Man

HONORING YOUR WIFE

*Let us not love in word or in tongue,
but in deed and in truth.*

1 JOHN 3:18

*He who follows righteousness and mercy
Finds life, righteousness, and honor.*

PROVERBS 21:21

*Set me as a seal upon your heart,
As a seal upon your arm;
For love is as strong as death,
Jealousy as cruel as the grave. . . .
Many waters cannot quench love,
Nor can the floods drown it.*

SONG OF SOLOMON 8:6–7

CLIMBING THE MOUNTAIN
OF MARRIAGE

———

Marriage is not just your average journey. It's more like climbing a mountain. Together. Early on, down in the foothills among the wildflowers, you start out side by side and hand in hand. But then the way becomes steep and barren. The flowers are far behind. There are a thousand obstacles on your trail. . . .

Unfortunately, too many climbers let their weariness get to their minds. They quit climbing. . . .

But those who stick with the climb, hanging onto the hand of that original partner—these are the ones who move higher. Sometimes one has to carry the other, but their commitment to reach the summit keeps them moving. Together. . . . And one day, on up ahead, they will reach the top. And there, in one another's arms, they'll celebrate the climb, sing to the world, and drink in the elixir of a climb well done.

Stay on the journey. You'll love the views ahead.

Stu Weber
Four Pillars of a Man's Heart

PROVIDING SPIRITUAL GUIDANCE
FOR YOUR FAMILY

Exhort one another daily, while it is called "Today," lest any of you be hardened through the deceitfulness of sin.

HEBREWS 3:13

Give unto the LORD the glory due to His name;
Worship the LORD in the beauty of holiness.

PSALM 29:2

The hour is coming, and now is, when the true worshipers will worship the Father in spirit and truth for the Father is seeking such to worship Him. God is Spirit, and those who worship Him must worship in spirit and truth.

JOHN 4:23–24

MEMORIES OF PRAISE AND LAUGHTER

God wants your home to be a center of worship. . . . How does that happen? . . .

Kneel. . . . Kneeling is an acknowledged point of submission. It is a way to bring anything under Christ's dominion. . . .

Sing. . . . Fill your house with song. . . .

Pray. . . while feeding on the Word. . . .

Sharing your answers to prayer and your discoveries in the Word becomes enriching to all.

What a heritage to pass on to our children . . . memories of home intertwined with memories of praise and laughter and song and the strong, undergirding arms of the living God.

Jack Hayford
Moments with Majesty

PROVIDING SPIRITUAL GUIDANCE
FOR YOUR FAMILY

The righteous man walks in his integrity;
His children are blessed after him.

PROVERBS 20:7

Let all bitterness, wrath, anger, clamor,
and evil speaking be put away from you,
with all malice. And be kind to one another,
tenderhearted, forgiving one another, even
as God in Christ forgave you.

EPHESIANS 4:31–32

All your children shall be taught by
*the L*ORD,
And great shall be the peace of your
children.

ISAIAH 54:13

DADS BRING HEALING

My oldest daughter was heartbroken. She had been cut from her gymnastics team, and her world had literally fallen apart. She came straight to my lap, and after we rocked in the rocking chair for thirty minutes, I told her how much God loves her heart and that He doesn't care anything about who stands on the balance beam and who doesn't.

Soon that little girl was okay because Daddy had touched her heart.

That night as I was tucking her into bed, I walked out of the room after we prayed together. Then I heard a little voice in the dark. "Daddy, thanks for tying my heart back together tonight.". . .

Dads are the ones who bring the healing hand of God when the world breaks their kids' hearts.

Joe White
(speech, Pittsburgh, Pennsylvania, 1996)

PROVIDING SPIRITUAL GUIDANCE
FOR YOUR FAMILY

*The fear of the LORD is the beginning
of wisdom;
A good understanding have all those who
do His commandments.*

PSALM 111:10

*The LORD gives wisdom;
From His mouth come knowledge
and understanding.*

PROVERBS 2:6

*We speak wisdom among those who are
mature, yet not the wisdom of this age,
nor of the rulers of this age, who are coming to nothing. But we speak the wisdom
of God in a mystery, the hidden wisdom
which God ordained before the ages for
our glory.*

1 CORINTHIANS 2:6–7

BE A WITNESS IN YOUR HOME

Your greatest witness for Jesus Christ is going to be at home. The people at home see you when you get mad. The people at home see you when you have a bad day on the job. The people at home see you when you are in the midst of trouble. Your greatest witness is going to be to your wife and children.

It's not enough to boast and brag to each other about how we've been changed. Our wives need to see that we've been changed. Our sons need to see that Daddy is different. Our daughters need to know that Jesus has come into our lives.

Go home! Just be a witness. . . . It starts at home.

Jeffrey Johnson
(*speech, Chicago, Illinois, 1997*)

PROVIDING SPIRITUAL GUIDANCE FOR YOUR FAMILY

If you confess with your mouth the Lord Jesus and believe in your heart that God has raised Him from the dead, you will be saved. For with the heart one believes unto righteousness, and with the mouth confession is made unto salvation.

ROMANS 10:9–10

[That we] speaking the truth in love, may grow up in all things into Him who is the head—Christ.

EPHESIANS 4:15

The house of the wicked will be overthrown,
But the tent of the upright will flourish.

PROVERBS 14:11

TELL THEM A THOUSAND TIMES

The best football coach in the past fifty years was Bud Wilkinson. His team won more than forty-five games in a row. His philosophy was: *Tell them how to do it. Tell them what you told them—and then tell them a thousand more times.*

In the same way we have to tell our children. Nowhere in the Bible does it say, don't give them too much of Jesus. What the Bible says is, tell them all day and then when you're done telling your children, tell your children's children. All your life you're supposed to be talking about Jesus. That's what men of God do. If we did that in our homes, our children would come alive.

We must get up at home and be the spiritual leaders. Model it, take part, demonstrate it. Let Jesus be first in your life and your children will imitate that.

Bill McCartney
(speech, Birmingham, Alabama ,1997)

PROVIDING SPIRITUAL GUIDANCE
FOR YOUR FAMILY

*In the fear of the LORD there is strong
    confidence,
And His children will have a place
    of refuge.*

PROVERBS 14:26

*Let Your work appear to Your servants,
And Your glory to their children.
And let the beauty of the LORD our God
    be upon us,
And establish the work of our hands for us.*

PSALM 90:16–17

*Every word of God is pure;
He is a shield to those who put their trust
    in Him.*

PROVERBS 30:5

FOLLOW THE GREAT COMMANDER

The Persian Gulf War was in full swing in early 1991, and the American people wanted to know how their boys were doing against Saddam Hussein's forces. As Schwarzkopf stood behind the podium in his army fatigues, surrounded by charts, maps, and satellite photos, he exuded a calm, secure presence that helped people all across the United States feel assured that victory would be swift and complete.

In a war, the commanding officer sets the tone. It is his plan that the troops must carry out, and it is his expertise that the fighting forces stake their lives on. . . . The officer in charge must watch over the battlefield, or the frontline people will battle in vain.

In your role as leader of your family, you are the last line of defense as you guard your kids and wife from the onslaught of the world. If you try to tackle that daunting task alone, you'll lose. You must align yourself under the leadership of the Great Commander!

Steve Farrar
Point Man

PROVIDING PROTECTION
FOR YOUR FAMILY

The LORD your God in your midst,
The Mighty One, will save;
He will rejoice over you with gladness,
He will quiet you with His love,
He will rejoice over you with singing.

ZEPHANIAH 3:17

Be strong and of good courage, do not fear
nor be afraid of them; for the LORD your
God, He is the One who goes with you. He
will not leave you nor forsake you.

DEUTERONOMY 31:6

You will keep him in perfect peace,
Whose mind is stayed on You,
Because he trusts in You.

ISAIAH 26:3

TEACHING FINANCIAL STEWARDSHIP

Here's a provocative question: Is it easier to train your children in financial principles around the coffee table or from your coffin? Obviously the correct answer is the first one. But why do so many parents wait until it's too late? . . .

Communicating about money promotes harmony and often avoids the bitterness that may be generated over money decisions. . . . It is an opportunity for Mom and Dad to begin to teach their children about budgeting, investment planning, estate planning and other financial responsibilities. Children can see their parents implementing and modeling wise financial stewardship. As they see their parents plan, they are more likely to plan in the future as well.

Ron Blue
Master Your Money

PROVIDING PROTECTION
FOR YOUR FAMILY

*The eyes of the L*ORD *run to and fro throughout the whole earth, to show Himself strong on behalf of those whose heart is loyal to Him.*

2 CHRONICLES 16:9

A word fitly spoken is like apples of gold In settings of silver.

PROVERBS 25:11

*The mercy of the L*ORD *is from everlasting to everlasting On those who fear Him, And His righteousness to children's children, To such as keep His covenant, And to those who remember His commandments to do them.*

PSALM 103:17–18

GOOD FATHERING HABITS

Understanding your significance to your children routinely affects how you use time and set priorities. If you know you are significant in your child's life, for instance, you schedule time to monitor her progress. You opt to attend a conference with your child's teacher instead of deferring to her mother—even if you have to rearrange your workday to do it. If your circumstances hamper good fathering habits, you look for alternatives that instead nurture your relationship with your children. I know men who would love to take up golf, or at least lower their handicap, but they decided against it—primarily because the time it takes to get good at golf would only eat into the already-too-few hours they have to relate with their children. They aren't perfect fathers, but they know their significance to their families.

Paul Lewis
Five Key Habits of Smart Dads

PROVIDING PROTECTION
FOR YOUR FAMILY

*I desire therefore that the men pray
everywhere, lifting up holy hands,
without wrath and doubting.*

1 TIMOTHY 2:8

*Remember the LORD, great and awesome,
and fight for your brethren, your sons,
your daughters, your wives, and your
houses.*

NEHEMIAH 4:14

*Your wife shall be like a fruitful vine
In the very heart of your house,
Your children like olive plants
All around your table.
Behold, thus shall the man be blessed
Who fears the LORD.*

PSALM 128:3–4

THE POWER OF A FATHER'S PRAYER

Never underestimate the power that comes when a parent pleads with God on behalf of a child. Who knows how many prayers are being answered right now because of the faithful ponderings of a parent ten or twenty years ago? God listens to thoughtful parents.

Praying for our children is a noble task. If what we are doing, in this fast-paced society, is taking us away from prayer time for our children, we're doing too much. There is nothing more special, more precious than time that a parent spends struggling and pondering with God on behalf of a child.

Max Lucado
Walking with the Savior

DISCIPLINING YOUR CHILDREN

A wise son makes a glad father,
But a foolish son is the grief of his
mother.

PROVERBS 10:1

Behold, children are a heritage from
the LORD,
The fruit of the womb is a reward.
Like arrows in the hand of a warrior,
So are the children of one's youth.
Happy is the man who has his quiver
full of them.

PSALM 127:3–5

Train up a child in the way he should go,
And when he is old he will not depart
from it.

PROVERBS 22:6

MOLDING YOUR CHILD'S WILL

The spirit of a child is a million times more vulnerable than his will. It is a delicate flower that can be crushed and broken all too easily (and even unintentionally). The spirit . . . relates to the self-esteem or the personal worth that a child feels. It is the most fragile characteristic in human nature. . . .

How then are we to shape the will while preserving the spirit intact? It is accomplished by establishing reasonable boundaries and enforcing them with love, but by avoiding any implications that the child is unwanted, unnecessary, foolish, ugly, dumb. . . . Don't keep scolding and nagging your children, making them angry and resentful. Rather, bring them up with the loving discipline the Lord Himself approves, with suggestions and godly advice.

James Dobson
The Strong-Willed Child

DISCIPLINING YOUR CHILDREN

*The father of the righteous will greatly
    rejoice,
And he who begets a wise child will
    delight in him.*

PROVERBS 23:24

*Correct your son, and he will give
    you rest;
Yes, he will give delight to your soul.*

PROVERBS 29:17

*Through wisdom a house is built,
And by understanding it is established.*

PROVERBS 24:3

LOVING DISCIPLINE

Love is the soil . . . in which truth comes alive. If you visualize truth as a seed, love is the soil in which the seed flourishes and produces growth. . . . There's no growth without truth. . . .

The thing that makes discipline effective is not a quick hand with the paddle. Discipline becomes effective when the child is moved by the fact that he has disappointed someone who loves him. Discipline outside of the context of love usually produces bitterness and resentment. Truth is easier to receive when it's surrounded by love.

Joseph C. Aldrich
Love for All Your Worth

DISCIPLINING YOUR CHILDREN

And you fathers, do not provoke your children to wrath, but bring them up in the training and admonition of the Lord.

EPHESIANS 6:4

Let deacons be the husbands of one wife, ruling their children and their own houses well.

1 TIMOTHY 3:12

He will turn
The hearts of the fathers to the children,
And the hearts of the children to their
*   fathers.*

MALACHI 4:6A

GIVING YOUR CHILDREN LIFE SKILLS

Effective discipline is [a] powerful way fathers instill in their children the life skills and principles that lead to success. Discipline teaches your children the realities of life's proper boundaries and the self-control to live happily within them. . . .

Yet each of your children is different, and each responds differently to different kinds of discipline. So study your children for what kind of discipline each child responds to most. . . .

As often as possible, set up disciplinary measures (or consequences) in advance of infractions. This helps your children to envision the impact of a bad choice and to take ownership of the outcome. If children can predict the disciplinary measures, then choose their behavior accordingly, you've given them a skill that will navigate them around all manner of bad consequences throughout life.

Paul Lewis
The Five Key Habits of Smart Dads

A MAN AND HIS CHURCH

HONOR AND SUPPORT
YOUR PASTOR

Let the elders who rule well be counted worthy of double honor, especially those who labor in the word and doctrine.

1 TIMOTHY 5:17

He who speaks from himself seeks his own glory; but he who seeks the glory of the One who sent Him is true, and no unrighteousness is in Him.

JOHN 7:18

Remember those who rule over you, who have spoken the word of God to you, whose faith follow, considering the outcome of their conduct.

HEBREWS 13:7

BEYOND THE HIGHEST REGARD

All Christians are called to practice honor. . . . God calls us to esteem, respect, and show deference to each other in the Body of Christ. When it comes to pastors, however, the Word of God says something unique. We read in 1 Thessalonians 5:12–13, "Now we ask you, brothers, to respect those who work hard among you, who are over you in the Lord and who admonish you. Hold them in the highest regard in love because of their work."

The phrase "hold them in the highest regard" is unusual in the original Greek of the New Testament in that it takes the adverb and triples its intensity. This verse could read, "Hold them *beyond* the highest regard in love.". . . Pastors are not to be esteemed for their office, degrees, age, or spiritual gifts, but "because of their work."

Dale Schlafer
Seven Promises of a Promise Keeper

HONOR AND SUPPORT
YOUR PASTOR

Obey those who rule over you, and be submissive, for they watch out for your souls, as those who must give account. Let them do so with joy and not with grief, for that would be unprofitable for you.

HEBREWS 13:17

All of you be submissive to one another, and be clothed with humility, for "God resists the proud, but gives grace to the humble."

1 PETER 5:5

Be subject to rulers and authorities, to obey, to be ready for every good work, to speak evil of no one, to be peaceable, gentle, showing all humility to all men.

TITUS 3:1–2

SERVING GOD'S SHEPHERDS

Our family was poor, but we always gave honor and respect—and the gifts we could afford—to our pastors. . . . I remember several times coming home from school and noticing that a rug was missing, some chairs were not in their usual place, or some other small items were gone. Instantly, I knew that the church had a new pastor who had moved into the parsonage. Mother had done some creative "housecleaning" on his behalf.

As a teenager, I came home from work one day to find that the first car I ever owned was gone. I asked Mother about my car, and she answered, "I noticed you've bought another car, so I gave your old one to the pastor.". . .

Men, it's time for us—not just our wives or our mothers—to show the way in blessing and honoring our pastors. We're the men of the church, and God has given us the mantle of leadership. He has also given us the high calling of serving His shepherds.

Jesse Miranda
Go the Distance

HONOR AND SUPPORT
YOUR PASTOR

You therefore, my son, be strong in the grace that is in Christ Jesus. And the things that you have heard from me among many witnesses, commit these to faithful men who will be able to teach others also.

2 TIMOTHY 2:1–2

I exhort first of all that supplications, prayers, intercessions, and giving of thanks be made for all men, for kings and all who are in authority, that we may lead a quiet and peaceable life in all godliness and reverence.

1 TIMOTHY 2:1–2

*Anxiety in the heart of man causes depression,
But a good word makes it glad.*

PROVERBS 12:25

TAKE THE PRESSURE OFF
THE PASTOR

Too many churches today are insulated, worried about the annual budget, membership quotes, and church growth. The burden invariably falls on the pastors—it's *expected* of them. But this must stop. The men and women of the church, as part of their time and treasure, must take some of the pressure off the pastors in these business-related activities so pastors can begin to attend to the more pressing business of ministering to the lost and addressing needs in the community.

Bill McCartney
Sold Out

HONOR AND SUPPORT
YOUR PASTOR

We have great joy and consolation in your love, because the hearts of the saints have been refreshed by you, brother.

PHILEMON 7

Let him who is taught the word share in all good things with him who teaches.

GALATIANS 6:6

LORD, who may abide in Your tabernacle?
Who may dwell in Your holy hill?
He who walks uprightly, and works
*   righteousness,*
And speaks the truth in his heart.

PSALM 15:1–2

THE JOY OF SERVANTHOOD

Several years ago a man in our church made an appointment to see me. I wondered what he wanted me to do for him. I'll never forget that appointment. Brent looked at me and said, "Pastor, I know you're so busy and the church is growing. God has been speaking to me in my devotions lately, and I would like to serve you."

I said, "Brent, what do you mean?"

He said, "I would be willing to give you a half a day every week. If you would just give the secretary a list of things for me to do, any dry cleaning you need to have picked up, or if you want your car washed—any errands you need to have done, I would like to do them, so you can have more time with your family and more time to serve the Lord."

With big tears streaming down his face, this dear brother was teaching me the joy of servanthood and the joy of receiving.

John Maxwell
(speech, Detroit, Michigan, 1997)

GIVING OF TIME AND RESOURCES

Since we are receiving a kingdom which cannot be shaken, let us have grace, by which we may serve God acceptably with reverence and godly fear.

HEBREWS 12:28

Let your light so shine before men, that they may see your good works and glorify your Father in heaven.

MATTHEW 5:16

And walk in love, as Christ also has loved us and given Himself for us, an offering and a sacrifice to God for a sweet-smelling aroma. Speaking to one another in psalms and hymns and spiritual songs, singing and making melody in your heart to the Lord, giving thanks always for all things to God the Father in the name of our Lord Jesus Christ.

EPHESIANS 5:2, 19–20

SPECTATOR CHRISTIANS

As the twentieth century draws to a close . . . we're seeing a disturbing trend among God's people. Too many are relinquishing their awesome responsibility for sharing in God's ministry. They've elected to stand on the sidelines while the pastor runs the whole show. In a sense, by abdicating this priceless birthright, they have accepted something far less for their lives than God intended. Rather than exercising their God-given gifts, creativity, and labor to build up the church, they've become passive "pew-sitters." These marginal Christians are functionally distanced from the daily activity of the church and emotionally detached from the needs, pain, and often hopelessness their chronic indifference has bred among God's shepherds.

Sadly, we live in a spectator society, where Christians and unbelievers alike grow up watching life from the periphery, conditioned to hire something done rather than doing it themselves.

Jesse Miranda
Go the Distance

GIVING OF TIME AND RESOURCES

As each one has received a gift, minister it to one another, as good stewards of the manifold grace of God.

1 PETER 4:10

Beloved, you do faithfully whatever you do for the brethren and for strangers, who have borne witness of your love before the church

3 JOHN 5-6

Whatever you do, do it heartily, as to the Lord and not to men, knowing that from the Lord yoiu will recieve the reward of the inheritance, for you serve the Lord Christ.

COLOSSIANS 3:23-24

GIVING GOD YOUR LEFTOVERS

Do you appreciate sloppy work? Neither do I. . . . And your boss certainly doesn't want sloppy work. . . .

God wants quality work from His stewards too. At His judgement seat, Jesus Christ is going to evaluate how well our time, talents and treasures were used for Him—whether they were used to produce quality work or thrown together junk.

Many people will give their boss top-quality work. . . . Why? Because their paycheck is in the boss's pocket. . . .

If people will do that for an earthly boss, what should we do for Jesus Christ? So the question is, are you giving God's kingdom a quality return on the time, talents, and treasure He has blessed you with? Or is God getting your leftovers?

Tony Evans
What a Way to Live!

GIVING OF TIME AND RESOURCES

*Honor the L*ORD *with your possessions,*
And with the firstfruits of all
*   your increase*

PROVERBS 3:9

Do not lay up for yourselves treasures on
earth, where moth and rust destroy and
where thieves break in and steal; but lay
up for yourselves treasures in heaven,
where neither moth nor rust destroys and
where thieves do not break in and steal.
For where your treasure is, there your
heart will be also.

3 JOHN 5-6

If there is among you a poor man of your
brethren, within any of the gates in your
land which the Lord you God is giving
you, yoiu shall not harden you heart nor
shut your hand from your poor brother
but you shall open your hand wide to him
and willingly lend him sufficient for his
needs, whatever he needs.

DEUTERONOMY 15:7-8

GIVING GLADLY

———

God definitely commands us to meet the needs of the saints and to fulfill the Great Commission. Thus, our purposes in giving are to give for the needy, for evangelism, and for disipleship in *our* Judea, *our* Samaria, and to the uttermost parts of the earth. Giving must be taken very seriously and decided upon consciously in order to fulfill the commands of Scripture. . . .

How much to give. . . is not as important as out attitude toward giving. . . .

In 2 Corinthians 8:9, Paul gave us the example of Christ to suggest the right attitude toward giving: "For you know the grace of our Lord Jesus Christ, that though He was rich, yet for your sakes He became poor that you through His poverty might become rich." So the attitude of giving must be one of cheerfulness and grace. Freely we have received, freely we must give.

Ron Blue
Master your Money

GIVING OF TIME AND RESOURCES

As we have many members in one body, but all the members do not have the same function, so we, being many, are one body in Christ, and individually members of one another.

ROMANS 12:4–5

There are diversities of gifts, but the same Spirit. There are differences of ministries, but the same Lord.

1 CORINTHIANS 12:4–5

Let no one seek his own, but each one the other's well-being.

1 CORINTHIANS 10:24

Yet it shall not be so among you; but whoever desires to become great among you shall be your servant. And whoever of you desires to be first shall be slave of all. For even the Son of Man did not come to be served, but to serve, and to give His life a ransom for many.

MARK 10:43–45

GOD OWNS EVERYTHING

You can't separate maturity and mammon. A man's checkbook and credit card statements are good barometers of his spiritual growth. I don't know about you, but that makes me uncomfortable! I'd much rather put the areas of my life into compartments and choose the ones to which God can have access. . . . Unfortunately, God doesn't operate that way. He's not interested in one or two or even three areas of [my] live; He wants all of me. . . .

God's Word teaches stewardship, which means managing things for someone else—the owner. Literally it means "the law of the house." When the master who owns the house is gone, he puts his possessions in the hands of a steward, and there are laws that govern the exercise of that steward's role.

Communism teaches that the government owns everything. Capitalism teaches that the individual owns everything. Biblical Christianity teaches that God owns everything.

E. Glenn Wagner
The Heart of a Godly Man

A MAN AND HIS BROTHERS

RECONCILED TO CHRIST

God was in Christ reconciling the world to Himself, not imputing their trespasses to them, and has committed to us the word of reconciliation. Now then, we are ambassadors for Christ, as though God were pleading through us: we implore you on Christ's behalf, be reconciled to God.

2 CORINTHIANS 5:19–20

Therefore remember that you, once Gentiles in the flesh—who are called Uncircumcision by what is called the Circumcision made in the flesh by hands— that at that time you were without Christ, being aliens from the commonwealth of Israel and strangers from the covenants of promise, having no hope and without God in the world. But now in Christ Jesus you who once were far off have been brought near by the blood of Christ.

EPHESIANS 2:11–13

GOD IS RECONCILING THE WORLD TO HIMSELF

God is working through Christ to reconcile the world to Himself. By faith in Christ and the forgiveness and cleansing He provides, a person is made right with God. God then places that person in the body of Christ [the church]. Though made of many different members, the body is the means God uses to carry the message of Christ to a lost world. With Christ as its Head, the body has the assignment of being ambassadors of Christ and appealing to all: "Be reconciled to God.". . .

Christ has already provided for our unity. Our problem is that we're not living in the reality of what He has provided. We're never commanded to produce unity. We're to keep or maintain the unity the Spirit has produced.

Raleigh Washington,
Glen Kehrein, and Claude V. King
Break Down the Walls

RECONCILED TO CHRIST

I, therefore, the prisoner of the Lord, beseech you to walk worthy of the calling with which you were called, with all lowliness and gentleness, with longsuffering, bearing one another in love, endeavoring to keep the unity of the Sprit in the bond of peace.

EPHESIANS 1:1–3

That their hearts may be encouraged, being knit together in love, and attaining to all riches of the full assurance of understanding, to the knowledge of the mystery of God, both of the Father and of Christ.

COLOSSIANS 2:2

Love never fails. But whether there are prophecies, they will fail; whether there are tongues, they will cease; whether there is knowledge, it will vanish away. And now abide faith, hope, love, these three; but the greatest of these is love.

1 CORINTHIANS 13:8, 13

RESTORING LOVE

Corrie Ten Boom was put in a German prison camp with her father and sister because they were trying to save Jewish people from the Nazis. They were tortured and her father and sister died, but Corrie was spared.

After the war she traveled and shared her testimony around the world. In one meeting she spotted the face of one of her prison guards. After the service the man came up to her and said, "I'm one of the guards who tortured you and your father and your sister. I've come here tonight because now I'm a Christian, and I want to ask you to forgive me."

Corrie said in her heart, "*Oh God, I can't forgive him.*" But at that very moment she could feel the love of God being poured into her heart. She said, "I stuck out my hand and I looked at that man, and I told him, 'I forgive you. And I know Jesus has saved you, praise God.'"

That is what reconciliation is all about. Only God's love can bring that kind of reconciliation.

Tom Claus
(speech, Buffalo, New York)

RECONCILED WITH
YOUR BROTHERS

For He Himself is our peace, who has made both one, and has broken down the middle wall of separation, having abolished in His flesh the enmity, that is, the law of commandments contained in ordinances, so as to create in Himself one new man from the two, thus making peace, and that He might reconcile them both to God in one body through the cross, thereby putting to death the enmity. And He came and preached peace to you who were afar off and to those who were near. For through Him we both have access by one Spirit to the Father.

EPHESIANS 2:14–18

You shall love the LORD your God with all your heart, with all your soul, with all your strength, and with all your mind, and your neighbor as yourself.

LUKE 10:27

If your brother sins against you, go and tell him his fault between you and him alone. If he hears you, you have gained your brother.

MATTHEW 18:15

TWO BIG GIANTS

Two big "giants" have been mocking Christians the way Goliath mocked Israel in King David's day. Racial hatred and bigotry, along with a factional spirit that judges and condemns other denominations or Christian traditions, have mocked Christian unity as an impossibility. God has called us to step forward like David. . . . And just as David depended on God for success, so we know that bringing down these two giants also depends upon God's power and guidance.

Raleigh Washington,
Glen Kehrein, and Claude V. King
Break Down the Walls

RECONCILED WITH
YOUR BROTHERS

There is neither Greek nor Jew, circumcised nor uncircumcised, barbarian, Scythian, slave nor free, but Christ is all and in all.

COLOSSIANS 3:11

Both He who sanctifies and those who are being sanctified are all of one, for which reason He is not ashamed to call them brethren.

HEBREWS 2:11

The LORD your God is God of gods and Lord of lords, the great God, mighty and awesome, who shows no partiality nor takes a bribe.

DEUTERONOMY 10:17

PRACTICE MAKES PERFECT

It's easy to be a Christian inside the church walls. It's safe in there. But when we leave the church and go out into the world determined to act biblically when it comes to race, it's easy to get intimidated and slip back into the old ways when our own race shows up.

It's easy when you go back to your community that has its own views on race to forget that you're part of a bigger family, the family of God. However, we might as well get used to each other being the color we are, because whatever color you are now, that is what you will be in heaven. . . .

Since what we will be then is what we are now, we had better learn to get along and live according to truth now. Practice makes perfect. Let's be the people of God that He has called us to be so that the broader culture has a model to look at in addressing the perpetual evil of racism.

Tony Evans
What a Way to Live

RECONCILED WITH
YOUR BROTHERS

If someone says, "I love God," and hates his brother, he is a liar; for he who does not love his brother whom he has seen, how can he love God whom he has not seen?

1 JOHN 4:20

Jesus said to him, "You shall love the Lord your God with all your heart, with all your soul and with all your mind. This is the first and great commandment. And the second is like it: You shall love your neighbor as yourself. On these two commandments hang all the Law and the Prophets."

MATTHEW 22:37–40

Peace to the brethren, and love with faith, from God the Father and the Lord Jesus Christ. Grace be with all those who love our Lord Jesus Christ in sincerity.

EPHESIANS 6:23–24

CROSSING BOUNDARIES

The racial problems in this country and throughout the world will not be solved without a lot of hard work. It's past time that we in the church take this mission of racial reconciliation seriously. If our Christianity doesn't have enough power to tear down walls of separation, why should the unbelieving world choose our gospel over any other religion?

The legacy of racism, racial tension, and separation offers Christians a unique opportunity—the chance to rise above the pretenders. The more we're able to cross the boundaries between groups of people, the more proof we have to offer the world of the truth of our gospel. And the more our Christianity can present a Body not divided like the rest of the world the louder we will be able to say with conviction that Jesus is, indeed, the answer.

John Perkins
Go the Distance

RECONCILED WITH
YOUR BROTHERS

*Behold, how good and how pleasant it is
For brethren to dwell together in unity!*

PSALM 133:1

*The glory which you gave Me I have given
them, that they may be one just as We are
one: I in them, and You in Me; that they
may be made perfect in one, and that the
world may know that You have sent Me,
and have loved them as You have loved
Me.*

JOHN 17:22–23

*In truth I perceive that God shows no par-
tiality. But in every nation whoever fears
Him and works righteousness is accepted
by Him.*

ACTS 10:34–35

WE'RE ALL GOOD TOGETHER

Some people say they don't see color. But unless they're blind, they're probably trying to be nice and say race is not an issue. In either case, they're wrong. For example, the authors of this [text], Phil Porter and Gordon England, are different racially. Both are okay, both are unique, but clearly they are not the same. Yet each adds flavor to the Body of Christ. Lettuce, tomatoes, cucumbers, and bell peppers are all different in appearance, taste, and texture, but all are good together in a salad. If this is hard to accept, run all your food through the blender for a month and you'll get the point.

Okay, then, what do we do? If we're convinced that God desires unity among all believers, each of us needs to reach out to brothers who are of different denominational or ethnic backgrounds.

Phil Porter and Gordon England
Seven Promises of a Promise Keeper

UNITY IN THE BODY

And the eye cannot say to the hand, "I have no need of you" nor again the head to the feet, "I have no need of you." No, much rather, those members of the body which seem to be weaker are necessary.

1 CORINTHIANS 12:21–22

Love does no harm to a neighbor; therefore love is the fulfillment of the law.

ROMANS 13:10

Finally, all of you be of one mind, having compassion for one another; love as brothers, be tenderhearted, be courteous; not returning evil for evil or reviling for reviling, but on the contrary, blessing, knowing that you were called to this, that you may inherit a blessing.

1 PETER 3:8–9

AN EMPOWERED, EFFICIENT TEAM

It's not my aim to reduce one of life's most profound principles to a sports metaphor. Still, I don't think it's a stretch to say that *team* began with God. Look in the Bible—team is *everywhere....*

The Bible is God's Play Book to instruct His people how to live, work, and minister together as a vital, empowered, efficient team....

Today teamwork remains the guiding principle of the church; God's blessing is bestowed in fullness and power only when His people are truly together. Unity, harmony, and togetherness in the church equals courage, faith, miracles, and new believers.

Bill McCartney
Sold Out

UNITY IN THE BODY

God is able to make all grace abound toward you, that you, always having all sufficiency in all things, may have an abundance for every good work.

2 CORINTHIANS 9:8

Many nations shall be joined to the LORD in that day, and they shall become My people. And I will dwell in your midst. Then you will know that the LORD of hosts has sent Me to you.

ZECHARIAH 2:11

That there should be no schism in the body, but that the members should have the same care for one another.

1 CORINTHIANS 12:25

LOVE ONE ANOTHER

Before Andrew Jackson became the seventh president of the Unites States, he served as a major general in the Tennessee militia. During the War of 1812 his troops reached an all-time low in morale. As a result they began arguing, bickering, and fighting among themselves. It is reported that Old Hickory called them all together and said, "Gentlemen! Let's remember, the enemy is over *there!*"

His sobering reminder would be an appropriate word for the church today. In fact, I wonder if Christ sometimes looks down at us and says with a sigh, "Christians, your Enemy is over there! Stop your infighting! Pull for one another. Support one another. Believe in one another. Care for one another. Pray for one another. Love one another."

Charles R. Swindoll
Hope Again

UNITY IN THE BODY

When you give a feast, invite the poor, the maimed, the lame, the blind. And you will be blessed, because they cannot repay you; for you shall be repaid at the resurrection of the just.

LUKE 14:13–14

We are His workmanship, created in Christ Jesus for good works, which God prepared beforehand that we should walk in them.

EPHESIANS 2:10

I have shown you in every way, by laboring like this, that you must support the weak. And remember the word of the Lord Jesus, that He said, "It is more blessed to give than to receive."

ACTS 20:35

CALLED TO A LIFE OF SERVICE

God has enlisted us in His navy and placed us on His ship. The boat has one purpose—to carry us safely to the other shore.

This is no cruise ship; it's a battleship. We aren't called to a life of leisure; we are called to a life of service. Each of us has a different task. Some, concerned with those who are drowning, are snatching people from the water. Others are occupied with the enemy, so they man the cannons of prayer and worship. Still others devote themselves to the crew, feeding and training the crew members.

Though different, we are the same. Each can tell of a personal encounter with the Captain, for each has received a personal call. He found us among the shanties of the seaport, and invited us to follow Him. Our faith was born at the sight of His fondness, and so we went. . . .

Though the battle is fierce, the boat is safe, for our captain is God.

Max Lucado
In the Grip of Grace

A MAN AND HIS WORLD

SHARING THE GOOD NEWS
WITH OTHERS

Go therefore and make disciples of all the nations, baptizing them in the name of the Father and of the Son and of the Holy Spirit, teaching them to observe all things that I have commanded you; and lo, I am with you always, even to the end of the age.

MATTHEW 28:19-20

Therefore God also has highly exalted Him and given Him the name which is above every name. That at the name of Jesus every knee should bow, and of those in heaven and of those on earth, and of those under the earth, and that every tongue should confess that Jesus Christ is Lord to the glory of God the Father.

PHILIPPIANS 2:9-11

I say to you, whoever confesses Me before men, him the son of Man also will confess before the angels of God. But he who denies Me before men will be denied before the angels of God.

LUKE 12:8-9

LEADING OTHERS TO CHRIST

A man new to the neighborhood was mowing his lawn with an ancient hand-pushed lawn mower. Across the street, a Christian neighbor was watching. He'd been praying for a way to reach his new friend for Christ, and when he saw the struggle with the antiquated lawn mower, a light bulb went on in his mind. *There was a brand new power mower in his garage!*

He wheeled it across the street and insisted that his new neighbor use it every time the grass needed mowing.

About eight weeks later, there was a knock at the door, and there stood the new neighbor, Bible in hand. Rather awkwardly, the neighbor pointed out his family tree, the marriage certificates at the front, and the burial notices at the back. Finally, he asked, "How can I be born again?" My Christian friend had the privilege of pointing his neighbor to Christ . . . all because of a lawnmower!

Joseph C. Aldrich
Gentle Persuasion

SHARING THE GOOD NEWS WITH OTHERS

I say to you that likewise there will be more joy in heaven over one sinner who repents than over ninety-nine just persons who need no repentance.

LUKE 15:7

For the Son of Man has come to seek and to save that which was lost.

LUKE 19:10

The Spirit of the Lord is upon Me,
Because He has anointed Me
To preach the gospel to the poor;
He has sent Me to heal the brokenhearted,
To proclaim liberty to the captives
And recovery of sight to the blind,
To set at liberty those who are oppressed.

LUKE 4:18

PLANING TO WIN THE LOST

If you are not regularly sharing your faith, you are not a joyous Christian, because God's greatest joy comes when people are won to Christ. Jesus said a party breaks out in heaven every time a sinner comes to Him.

For most of us, effective evangelism doesn't just happen. It has to be a planned part of our lives. A man we know told us he joined the local Rotary Club a few years ago for the express purpose of being around lost people so he could witness to them. This friend planned at least one witnessing occasion every week, so that at the end of a year he had witnessed to at least fifty-two people.

What decision have you made to place yourself next to non-Christians so you can win them to Christ?

Tony Evans
Seasons of Love

SHARING THE GOOD NEWS
WITH OTHERS

Whoever confesses Me before men, him I will also confess before My Father who is in heaven. But whoever denies Me before men, him I will also deny before My Father who is in heaven.

MATTHEW 10:32–33

Behold, I stand at the door and knock. If anyone hears My voice and opens the door, I will come in to him and dine with him, and he with Me.

REVELATION 3:20

He who has the Son has life; he who does not have the Son of God does not have life.

1 JOHN 5:12

LET'S WAKE UP!

I have a recurring dream. . . . It's a picture of the world if Jesus had free rein in our lives. It's a picture of how God intended our planet to look, with humanity so red hot, so electrified by Jesus that the landscape is visibly transformed. What *would* society look like? For one, the word "lukewarm" wouldn't exist. Everyone would always be talking about God, praising Him for His miraculous blessings. . . . Network television shows and prime-time programming would be dominated by stories about Jesus. . . .

In the Old Testament, pagan nations feared the God of the Israelites. Today, how many unbelievers fear the God of the Christians? . . . If you wonder why God has become increasingly irrelevant in our culture, it's because Christians look exactly like the culture. The church has become like the world—lukewarm. . . .

Isn't it time we became the people of God? We have been given the legacy of inexhaustible life from the only One who conquered death. Isn't it time to wake from our slumber and lay hold of this treasured birthright?

Bill McCartney
Sold Out

SHARING THE GOOD NEWS
WITH OTHERS

Let your light so shine before men, that they may see your good works and glorify your father in heaven.

MATTHEW 5:16

And He said to them, "Go into all the world and preach the gospel to every creature. He who believes and is baptized will be saved; but he who does not believe will be condemned."

MARK 16:15–16

If anyone serves Me, let him follow Me; and where I am, there My servant will be also. If anyone serves Me, him My Father will honor.

JOHN 12:26

SHOW THEM JESUS

Your job in the workplace is to help people see what being a child of God might look like. My second tour in Vietnam, I didn't have to go back. I had already done one tour. I talked to my dear wife, Sarah, and she said, "It's over, you've already lost too many friends. I've gone to too many funerals. Why would you want to go back?"

I said, "Because it's hopeless. These guys are in a thankless, hopeless situation. My job, if God permits, is to go back and give them hope."

When I got there we had a chaplain, a little pug-nosed, energetic guy who loved marines and loved troops almost as much as he loved Jesus. Jerry Morrison and I prayed and by the Grace of God over 300 young marines came to know Christ as their Savior. *That* was the purpose of that second tour.

Tom Hemingway
(speech, Buffalo, New York, 1997)

SHARING THE GOOD NEWS
WITH OTHERS

For God so loved the world that he gave His only begotten Son, that whoever believes in Him should not perish, but have everlasting life.

JOHN 3:16

The Lord is not slack concerning His promise, as some count slackness, but is long suffering toward us, not willing that any should perish but that all should come to repentance.

2 PETER 3:9

And they went out and preached everywhere, the Lord working with them and confirming the word through the accompanying signs.

MARK 16:20

WALK YOUR POST

May Christian men become truth-tellers—even when the truth stings.

Does the warrior in you stand up when you should? Do you defend the truth in your personal conversations? With your children? With your neighbors? With your co-workers? Do people around you know where you stand? Don't get me wrong. I'm not asking anyone to be ugly, overbearing, or arrogant. But I do think it more than reasonable that warriors wear their uniforms in public. I understand that it's easier to wear your "civvies" and remain anonymous, but that is not why your heavenly Commander stationed you on this planet. Walk your post. And say the hard thing when it's right and appropriate.

Stu Weber
Four Pillars of a Man's Heart

REACHING OUT TO THE WORLD

Beloved, let us love one another, for love is of God; and everyone who loves is born of God and knows God. He who does not love does not know God, for God is love.

1 JOHN 4:7–8

This is My commandment, that you love one another as I have loved you. Greater love has no one than this, than to lay down one's life for his friends. You are My friends if you do whatever I command.

JOHN 14:12–13

The work of righteousness will be peace, and the effect of righteousness, quietness and assurance forever.

ISAIAH 32:17

CRISIS CREATES CHALLENGE

The Chinese character for the word *crisis* is a combination of two other Chinese characters. One is the character for danger, and the other is the character for opportunity. Our world is in a state of crisis. Our nation is in a state of crisis. . . . We are surrounded by crisis. Crisis creates challenge because with the danger of crisis come the opportunities crisis creates for peacemaking.

Never in human history have there been more opportunities to be a witness for Christ. The danger most men face is becoming so overwhelmed by the scope of the need that they do nothing. In order to become effective as witnesses, we need to sort through the multitude of opportunities available and focus our limited time, energy, and resources where we can make our greatest peacemaking contribution.

Dr. Bob Beltz
Daily Disciplines for the Christian Man

REACHING OUT TO THE WORLD

Let a man so consider us, as servants of Christ and stewards of the mysteries of God. Moreover it is required in stewards that one be found faithful.

1 CORINTHIANS 4:1–2

Assuredly, I say to you inasmuch as you did not do it to one of the least of these, you did not do it unto Me.

MATTHEW 25:45

Let us not grow weary while doing good, for in due season we shall reap if we do not lose heart. Therefore, as we have opportunity, let us do good to all, especially to those who are of the household of faith.

GALATIANS 6:9–10

THE CAUSE OF CHRIST NEVER DIES

A man was made for something outside of himself. A man was made for something beyond. That's why so many of us draw a disproportionate sense of achievement from our jobs, ordinary as they may be. And that's why so many newly-retired men suddenly find life tasteless and empty. Through all their years, they have completely attached their masculine identity to the Wedgwood Lumber Company or the Pushpenny National Bank. . . . Then, when they have worked their thirty or forty years and collected their gold watch, it's done. Their job is over, and so is their reason for living! . . .

What a needless tragedy! For the cause of Christ *never* dies. Never lessens its call on a man's life. Never ceases to throb with urgency as time rushes on a short track toward eternity.

The cause is eternal. The kingdom is out there. Kingdom deeds await doing in the borrowed might of the Almighty.

Stu Weber
Tender Warrior

His lord said to him, "Well done, good and faithful servant; you were faithful over a few things, I will make you ruler over many things. Enter into the joy of your lord."

MATTHEW 25:21

Give and it will be given to you; good measure, pressed down, shaken together, and running over will be put into your bosom. For with the same measure that you use, it will be measured back to you.

LUKE 6:38

There is one who scatters, yet increases more; and there is one who withholds more than is right, but it leads to poverty. The generous soul will be made rich, and he who waters will also be watered himself.

PROVERBS 11:24–25

A NOVEL IDEA

In some small New England towns, the most popular tourist attraction is the local cemetery. As you walk along and read the centuries-old gravestones, you'll see humorous sayings (apparently written by less-than-generous spouses), sad words telling of the death of a child or other loved one, and serious messages with profound meaning.

Have you ever wondered what will be placed on your burial marker? When you die, how will you have spent the one life God has entrusted to you? What motivates you day by day? Is it a desire to be liked or to be happy? Will people say that you grabbed hold of everything you could?

For us Christians, God has a different plan. He says that it's in giving that we receive, in losing that we gain. What a novel idea! Instead of living me-centered lives, we're called by God to other-centered living. And when we accept that call, it's amazing what He can and will do through one person, or one church, to reach out to a hurting world.

Gregg Lewis
The Power of a Promise Kept

REACHING OUT TO THE WORLD

Those who are wise shall shine like the brightness of the firmament, and those who turn many to righteousness like the stars forever and ever.

DANIEL 12:3

Most assuredly, I say to you, he who believes in Me, the works that I do he will do also; and greater works than these he will do because I go to My Father.

JOHN 14:12

But grow in the grace and knowledge of our Lord and Savior Jesus Christ. To Him be the glory both now and forever Amen.

2 PETER 3:18

GOD'S GREAT COMMISSION

It's not our love, our gospel that's going to change anyone's life. It's God's love, God's Good News of salvation. And it's only by His love in and through us, communicating His gospel message, that men, women, youth, and children will be saved. . . .

What's the secret of being a promise keeper, a man of integrity who's influencing his world for God's glory? It's not us, doing our own little thing, in our own power. It's God at work in and through us. . . .

Imagine what the world will be like if you and I join hands with millions of other brothers in Christ (and sisters, too) and promise to stay true to God's Great Commandment and Great Commission for the rest of our lives! We'll witness the greatest "season of refreshing" in all history!

Luis Palau
Go the Distance

ACKNOWLEDGMENTS

Grateful acknowledgment is made to the following publishers and copyright holders for permission to reprint copyrighted material:

Joseph C. Aldrich, *Love for All Your Worth* (Sisters, Or.: Multnomah Books, 1993).

Joseph C. Aldrich, *Reunitus: Building Bridges to Each Other Through Prayer Summits* (Sisters, Or.: Multnomah Books, 1994).

Joseph C. Aldrich, *Gentle Persuasion* (Sisters, Or.: Multnomah Books, 1974).

Bob Beltz, *Daily Disciplines for the Christian Man: Practical Steps to an Empowered Spiritual Life* (Colorado Springs: NavPress, 1993).

Ron Blue, *Master Your Money: A Step by Step Plan for Financial Freedom* (Nashville: Thomas Nelson Publishers, 1993).

Wellington Boone, *Breaking Through* (Nashville: Broadman and Holman, 1996).

Bill Bright et al., *Seven Promises of a Promise Keeper* (Colorado Springs: Focus on the Family Publishing, 1994).

James Dobson, *The Strong-Willed Child* (Wheaton, Ill.: Tyndale House Publishing, 1992).

Tony Evans, *What a Way to Live: Running All of Life by the Kingdom Agenda* Nashville: Word Publishing, 1997).

Tony and Lois Evans, *Seasons of Love: A Daily Devotional for Couples* (Nashville: Word Publishing, 1998).

Steve Farrar, *Point Man: Taking New Ground* (Sisters, Or.: Multnomah Books, 1996).

Jack Hayford, *Moments with Majesty* (Sisters, Or.: Multnomah Books, 1990).

Gregg Lewis, *The Power of a Promise Kept* (Colorado Springs: Focus on the Family Publishing, 1995).

Paul Lewis, *The Five Key Habits of Smart Dads: A Powerful Strategy for Successful Fathering* (Grand Rapids: Zondervan Publishing House, 1994).

Max Lucado, *Just Like Jesus* (Nashville: Word Publishing, 1998).

Max Lucado, *In the Grip of Grace* (Nashville: Word Publishing, 1996).

Max Lucado, *Walking with the Savior* (Nashville: Word Publishing, 1997).

Bill McCartney, *Sold Out: Becoming Man Enough to Make a Difference* (Nashville: Word Publishing, 1997).

William Carr Peel, *What God Does When Men Pray* (Colorado Springs:NavPress, 1993).

Gary Smalley, *The Key to Your Child's Heart* (Nashville: Word Publishing, 1992).

Gary Smalley, *Making Love Last Forever* (Nashville: Word Publishing, 1996).

Charles R. Swindoll, *Hope Again* (Nashville: Word Publishing, 1997).

John Trent et al., *Go the Distance: The Making of a Promise Keeper* (Colorado Springs: Focus on the Family, 1996).

E. Glenn Wagner, *The Heart of a Godly Man: Practical Disciplines for a Man's Spiritual Life* (Chicago: Moody Press, 1997).

E. Glenn Wagner, Ph.D., with Dietrich Gruen, *Strategies for a Successful Marriage: A Study Guide for Men* (Colorado Springs: NavPress, 1994).

Raleigh Washington, Glen Kehrein, and Claude V. King, *Break Down the Walls* (Chicago: Moody Press, 1997).

Stu Weber, *Tender Warrior: God's Intention for a Man* (Sisters, Or.: Multnomah Books, 1993).

Stu Weber, *Four Pillars of a Man's Heart: Bringing Strength into Balance* (Sisters, Or.: Multnomah Books, 1997).

Ravi Zacharias, *Cries of the Heart* (Nashville: Word Publishing, 1998).